TROOPING THE COLOUR

TROOPING
THE COLOUR

A History of
The Sovereign's Birthday Parade

Michael Gow

Foreword by
Field Marshal His Royal Highness
The Prince Philip, Duke of Edinburgh,
KG, KT, OM, GBE, QSO,
Colonel Grenadier Guards,
Senior Colonel Household Division

SOUVENIR PRESS

First published 1988 by Souvenir Press Ltd,
43 Great Russell Street, London WC1B 3PA
and simultaneously in Canada
New Edition 1989

ISBN 0 285 62906 9

Photoset and printed in Great Britain by
Redwood Burn Limited,
Trowbridge, Wiltshire

Frontispiece

HM Queen Elizabeth The Queen Mother, accompanied by TRH The Princess of Wales and
Prince William, passes through Number 3 Guard on to Horse Guards Parade to attend the 1988
ceremony. *PRO HQ London District*

Photograph on page 6: *PRO HQ London District*

Dedicated by Gracious Permission
to
Her Majesty The Queen
Colonel-in-Chief of the Regiments of
The Household Cavalry and Foot Guards

Most countries have great military parades to mark some important event in their history. The best known is probably the display of military might in front of Lenin's mausoleum in Moscow on the anniversary of the October Revolution. True to the pragmatic nature of the British, the only annual military parade in London is nothing more than a celebration of the birthday of the Sovereign by the Household Troops. As a wise precaution against the uncertainties of our weather, it takes place on the official, and not on the actual date of the birthday.

Furthermore, all the troops taking part are dressed in Full Dress uniform, which traces its design back to the early 18th century. It is all very colourful, but it disguises the fact that the Guardsmen are also fully operational soldiers with battalions taking their turn of duty with the British Army in Germany, in Northern Ireland and anywhere else that British troops are required to serve. Only a few years ago battalions of both the Scots and the Welsh Guards were on very active service in the Falkland Islands.

The parade itself is familiar to most people, but even for those who are intimately involved in its organisation, its origin and development probably remain shrouded in mystery. General Sir Michael Gow has written a fascinating account of how it all started and of how wars and personalities, weapons and the weather have shaped the pattern of the parade we know today.

The author is uniquely qualified to write about this military spectacle. He joined the Scots Guards in 1942 and served in the Army for 44 years. He has commanded the Escort to the Colour on the Birthday Parade and Guards on three other occasions, he has appeared mounted twice as Regimental Adjutant, once as Adjutant in Brigade Waiting, and once as the Officer Commanding the Troops Lining the Mall.

In the early days of the parade all military officers had ridden since childhood. This no longer applies and in these mechanical days it must be a cause of considerable concern to those whose duties require them to ride a horse on this one occasion in the year.

When I first took part I was fortunate enough to have been playing polo for some years, so that the prospect of getting on to a horse was rather less daunting, but even so there is a great difference between polo kit and a pony of 15.2 hands and full dress uniform on a horse of 17 hands. Furthermore on the day itself as opposed to the rehearsals, there are a lot of people about and there is an air of excitement which tends to affect the horses as much as the riders. To add to the anxiety, it is only too obvious that the ground is a great deal harder, and more slippery, than the turf of a polo field.

I have ridden the course on several occasions and it is never quite the same. Things don't necessarily go badly, or obviously, wrong, but odd things are liable to happen. On one occasion after taking the salute at a second rehearsal, I was coming back up the Mall to the Palace but, instead of following the bands round to the right of the Victoria Memorial, for some reason which escapes me, I kept to the normal traffic route and went the other way. No harm was done, but I expect it caused a certain amount of consternation among those riding behind me.

Of all the parades that I have witnessed, the only time I was able to see it properly was on my very first outing when I rode dressed as a Field Marshal and wearing a cocked hat. This was in 1953, before I was appointed Colonel of the Welsh Guards and therefore not required to wear the Guards officer's bearskin cap. The snag about wearing a bearskin while mounted on a horse is that it is rather top-heavy and in order to keep it firmly anchored against gusts of wind and unexpected movements of the horse, it is advisable to let it sit as low on the head as possible without being completely blinded. The consequence is that while there is a clear view downwards, the view straight ahead is through a fringe of fur which makes everything look as if it were taking place in torrential rain.

For anyone not accustomed to wearing a bearskin regularly, its weight can be quite a trial and it feels somewhat insecure. Soon after I was married, I arrived at Royal Lodge for the weekend, and as I strolled out into the garden I heard fearful imprecations coming from the middle of a large rhododendron. I approached with caution to be astonished by the sight of a figure under what appeared to be a black tea-cosy. It was not many years before I fully appreciated the value of my father-in-law's practice of getting used to his bearskin in preparation for the parade.

I believe that the popularity of the parade is due to the basic simplicity of the sequence of events and the curiously intimate nature of the whole thing. Riding down the Mall at a walking pace allows plenty of time to see individuals in the crowd and for the spectators to enjoy the colourful spectacle and to see more of the participants than a blur in a passing car. Of all the regiments of the Army we inevitably see more of the Guards than any other, so that the men on parade are familiar figures and many of the officers are known personally or are sons of former officers. The Birthday Parade has always been a typically British mixture of impeccable ceremonial with a very human and personal purpose.

Contents

Photograph: *PRO HQ London District*

Acknowledgements

The quotations and photographs from the Royal Archives are reproduced by Gracious Permission of Her Majesty The Queen.

I am grateful to the Major General Commanding the Household Division, his predecessors, and the Headquarters of the Household Division, Household Cavalry and Regiments of Foot Guards for their help and advice; to the Curator of the Household Cavalry Museum, Windsor, and the Director and Curator of the Guards Museum, Wellington Barracks, to Major Harold Schofield, formerly Welsh Guards, the Divisional Archivist, and to Miss Alex Ward of the Army Historical Branch, for their help in research; to the late Lady Osborn for her kind permission to quote from a letter of Lieutenant Colonel Sir George Osborn, Bt.; to Lieutenant Colonel Rodney Bashford, formerly Grenadier Guards, and the Garrison Sergeant Majors London District for their suggestions and contributions; to the Duke of Wellington for allowing me to reproduce the painting at Stratfield Saye by Henry Barrand of Queen Victoria in her phaeton; to the Viscount Montgomery of Alamein for allowing me to reproduce the letter by his father to the Major General; to Mr E. J. Collings and the National Army Museum for their permission to reproduce photographs from the Mrs Albert Broom and Fairhaven Collections respectively; to Lieutenant Colonel Trevor Morris, The Blues and Royals, and the Staff of the Public Information Office, Headquarters London District, for their help and production of illustrations; to the Imperial War Museum, the British Museum, S & G Press Agency, Illustrated London News Picture Library, The Photo-Source/Keystone, Express Newspapers, Times Newspapers, and PA Photos, for permission to reproduce copyright photographs and illustrations; to the Public Record Office for permission to quote from Crown Copyright material; to Macmillan Publishing Company, New York, for permission to quote from *A King's Story* (Copyright © 1951) and *A Family Album* (Copyright © 1960) by HRH The Duke of Windsor, published by Cassell & Co.; to Mr B. Harwood, formerly The Life Guards, for allowing me to draw on his unique research on the history of Horse Guards Building; to Mr Oliver Everett, LVO, Librarian and Assistant Keeper of the Queen's Archives,

Miss Jane Langton, LVO, Miss Elizabeth Cuthbert, LVO, and Miss Frances Dimond of the Royal Archives for their patience and unstinting advice; to Miss Tessa Harrow whose professional expertise in editing and kindness to the author were invaluable; and finally to Miss Penny Lewis who typed and retyped the text.

J. M. G.

Preface

The first historical account of the Sovereign's Birthday Parade was written and published as a supplement to the *Guards Magazine* in 1979. In 1988 I brought it up to date and it was first published as a book entitled *Trooping the Colour: A History of the Sovereign's Birthday Parade.*

This second edition has been further updated and includes additional material. I have added to the Appendices so that they provide short histories of the Queen's Guard, Horse Guards and Horse Guards Parade, and of the Bands and Music of the Foot Guards. I hope that this will be of interest to Guardsmen, past and present, and to those who witness an event of national importance, seen worldwide by millions on television.

The following explanation of the Colours may be helpful to the reader:

In the eighteenth century, when the Colours of a Regiment were carried in battle and formed a rallying point, it was necessary for them to be known and recognised by their soldiers, and for that reason they were marched (or 'trooped') slowly along the ranks.

Before 1700 every Company of a Regiment had its own Colour, but this number was reduced and by 1751 there were two, as now, for each Battalion—the Queen's and the Regimental Colours. In the Foot Guards the former is crimson (while the latter is the Union) and is carried only by a Guard mounted on the Queen, the Duke of Edinburgh, Queen Elizabeth The Queen Mother, or when any of these are present; by the Queen's Guard at Buckingham Palace when Her Majesty is in official residence in London, on Royal Anniversaries and when it is formed into a Guard of Honour.

It is the Queen's Colour which is trooped in London, while elsewhere it is the Regimental Colour unless the Queen is present in person. Both Colours are replaced every ten years (Authority: HQ Household Division letter 1500 of 30 August, 1974).

The three senior Regiments, uniquely, also have State Colours: that of the Grenadier Guards is the 'Queen's Company Colour, the Royal Standard of the Regiment', and it certainly existed when Charles II was King. It bears no battle honours but is emblazoned with the Royal Cypher and in each corner with the emblems of the United Kingdom. On the accession of a Sovereign, a new Royal Standard is presented to the Queen's Company. On the second anniversary of his accession, on 26 June 1832, however, William IV presented also a new Colour pike which is still in use and which has a three-dimensional silver gilt ornamented top. With the exception of this Colour, which is in the possession of the Regiment, when they are replaced, the old Royal Standards are lodged in the Queen's Guard Chamber at Windsor Castle.

This Standard should not be confused with the Queen's Company Colour or Flag which is a small replica. Every Foot Guards Company has its own Flag, but this one is unique: at the funeral of the Sovereign it is placed personally by the new Sovereign upon the top of the coffin where it remains *in perpetuo*, a replacement being provided by the Regiment.

The Coldstream Guards possess two State Colours which are carried on occasions analogous to those upon which that of the Grenadiers is taken out. No record has been found of why or when they were presented and both are slightly different, the Second bearing the battle honours of the Crimean War in addition to those of Lincelles, Talavera, Barossa, Egypt, Peninsula and Waterloo, which are emblazoned on the First.

In the case of the Scots Guards, at Windsor in 1899 Queen Victoria, as a personal gift, presented a State Colour which bears twelve battle honours. It is carried by Guards of Honour of the Regiment, not furnished by the Queen's Guard, which are mounted on State occasions at which Her Majesty is present.

Both Regiments of Household Cavalry—The Life Guards and The Blues and Royals—have a Royal Standard and three Squadron Standards of crimson damask, with battle honours in gold embroidery. These are kept by the Mounted Regiment at Knightsbridge Barracks in London. The Blues and Royals also have a Guidon resulting from the amalgamation with the Royal Dragoons in 1969, which is usually kept wherever the Regiment is stationed.

Unlike the Infantry, in the Household Cavalry the Standards are carried by Warrant or Senior Non Commissioned Officers, and a Royal Standard is always carried when a Sovereign's Escort accompanies the Queen, as is the case on the Birthday Parade.

With the exception of the State Colours of the Coldstream Guards, for which there is no evidence, all other Colours—State, Queen's and Regimental—and all Standards are consecrated[1] and therefore treated with great

---

[1] The origins of the Colours being consecrated are uncertain. Gerat Barry in *A Discourse on Military Discipline*, 1634, writes: 'After choysinge his officers as aforesaid, before he (Captaine of a Companie of Infanterie) marches with the same, he is first to cause the Colores to be blest, and afterwards deliver the same to the Alferis (Ensign).'

Dr Dakins (1767–1850) was Deputy Chaplain to the 1st Guards in 1793 and Principal Chaplain to the Forces and Chaplain to the Brigade of Guards 1830–44. He was also responsible for the building of the Guards Chapel at Wellington Barracks which was opened in May

respect by soldiers and civilians alike, the former saluting and the latter uncovering when they pass, while Her Majesty bows her head as she stands on the dais at the Birthday Parade and her Colour and Standard are carried before her. They represent the history, traditions and *esprit de corps* of their soldiers of all ranks.

1838. He wrote: 'No regulations, in my recollection, ever did exist for the performance of that ceremony (of consecration). The custom was prevalent but the manner varied.' (*Standards, Guidons and Colours* by Edwards. Gale and Polden, 1952, p. 114.) The earliest reference in Queen's Regulations was in 1867.

Origins to 1914

The ceremony of Trooping the Colour, held on the occasion of The Queen's Birthday, is a parade that is famous worldwide, but its origins and its history are perhaps less well known. The earliest traceable orders relating to Trooping the Colour are contained in the Order Books of the Grenadier and Coldstream Guards, that of the former, dated 19 February 1749, reading:

> According to a former Order the Colours of the King's guard when returned to the Parade are always to be lodged in form, two Sergeants, the Fifers, two Drummers and eight half-files of Grenadiers[1] to troop the Colours; the remaining part of the guard is not to be dismissed until they are joined by those who Trooped the Colours, who are to return in the same Order, excepting only that their Bayonets are to be returned . . .

The Coldstream Guards' Order for 18 February 1749 records: 'the Colours be always trooped at the Mounting and Dismounting of the guards, unless in very bad weather.' An order of HRH The Duke of Cumberland, dated 15 May 1755, relating to the parading of Guards in Quarters or Garrison, whenever the Guard mounts with Colours, is also relevant:

> As soon as the Colours [sic] are handed out to the Ensign . . . he troops his detachment to the Parade. When he comes to one of the Flanks of the Parade, he is to face his detachment to the Right or Left, the men marching between the Flanks and the Ensign in front of the line of officers, each of whom are to pay the proper respect to the Colours by pulling off their hats as they pass . . .

The public duties furnished by the Foot Guards paraded on the Horse Guards Parade daily until the spring of 1817. In that year the annual change of quarters took place on 25 February and the duties seem to have used their

---

[1] This refers to the Grenadier (or assault) company, and not to the Grenadier Guards as a Regiment.

private parade grounds until 1 April. From 1817 to 1856 the custom appears to have been to parade and march off the duties from Horse Guards Parade from April to September, with some variation from 1 April to 1 May, but from 1859 it became established for this to happen from 1 May to the day of The Queen's Birthday Parade only, as is the present practice.

The first traceable mention of the Sovereign's Birthday being 'kept' is an order in the Grenadier Guards' Book dated 30 November 1748: 'Ordered by the Field Officer, 2 Sergeants, 2 Corporals and 40 Private Men be added to the King's Guard on Friday next being the day appointed for keeping His Majesty's Birthday.' It is possible that at this time the Duties were larger because of the extra men required for the State Balls which were held on the occasions of the birthdays of the King and the Queen.

According to the Coldstream Order Book for 17 June 1768, the King ordered the Grenadier Battalion (i.e. the Grenadier Companies of the Foot Guards) to mount guard 'on the day which His Majesty's birthday is ordered to be kept', but this was not necessarily the actual day.[2] And in the Books of all three Regiments in the latter part of the century there were orders for officers' dress being ready for the King's Birthday.[3]

On 31 May, 1805, 'the Field Officer in Waiting having received the command of HRH the Commander-in-Chief directs that the five companies of Grenadiers now in London shall parade in St James's Park in Full Dress and white Gaiters at the usual hour for Guard on Tuesday, 4 June in Honour of HM's Birthday. The Grenadiers of the 3rd Brigade will furnish the Guards that day. The Coldstream Band will attend.' (Coldstream Guards' Order Book.)

In 1806, on 3 June, 'The General and Staff Officers belonging to the District who are resident in or near London are requested to meet the Duke of Cambridge on the Parade at the Horse Guards at 10 o'clock on the morning of the next Anniversary of the King's Birthday, to be fully dressed in Embroidered Cloths.'[4]

From 1807 to 1810 orders were issued for Parades on the birthdays of both the King and the Queen, the one in June and the other in January. They were not held from 1811 to 1820 because of King George III's illness, except in 1813 for the Queen, but from the accession of King George IV they became, with a few exceptions and notably the two World Wars, an annual event. King

---

[2] For example, Lt. Col. Sir George Osborn Bt, 3rd Guards 1765–1786, writing to his brother, the Ambassador at the Court of Dresden, 24 May 1768: 'This letter will hasten, I hope, your return to London as I could wish to have you here before the Birthday Review which is put off till 25th June. As our Review cannot be till ten days after the Birthday, you will find me in the Grenadier Battalion . . .' And the Birthday of George IV was 'kept' on 7 May 1830, while the actual day was 12 August, by which time the King was dead.

[3] An example is an order in the Scots Guards' Book dated 2 June 1793: 'His Royal Highness the Duke of Gloucester orders the Guards to mount in new clothing on the 4th June in honour of His Majesty's Birthday but the Brigade of Guards are afterwards to do all duty in the clothing of this year until further orders.'

[4] Coldstream Guards' Order Book.

Guard Mounting. 'A Perspective View of the Parade in St James's Park, showing the New Buildings for the Horse Guards, the Treasury, and the Admiralty Office.' Line engraving by and after J. Maurer, published by Robert Wilkinson, London, *c.* 1752. *Fairhaven Collection*

William IV revived the Queen's Parade, the detail of which seems to have been precisely the same as that for the King.

The link between the Birthday Parade and Guard Mounting is illustrated by the Regimental order of the Grenadier Guards published 22 May 1839:

> The General Commanding in Chief will attend the Guard Mounting at 10 o'clock a.m. tomorrow, the anniversary of Her Majesty's birthday, on the parade in St James's Park. The flank companies of the Foot Guards will parade with the Guards on that occasion. The Household Cavalry Guard will form on the right of the line. The troops will march past in slow and quick time after which the ceremony of Guard Mounting will take place.

There is no record of Queen Victoria ever taking the salute in London, but during his lifetime the Prince Consort was sometimes present:

> Albert came to breakfast dressed in his uniform for the Birthday Parade, this being the day on which my birthday is officially kept. At ¼ to 10 I drove quite *in cog* with Bertie & Ly Lyttelton, in a small green Chariot round by the Bird Cage Walk, to the Horse Guards, where we had an admirable view of the Parade, & without being *found out*. Bertie stood at the open window, transfixed with delight, & though it lasted long, he was wretched when all was over. I saw my beloved Albert ride up with Uncle

Guard Mounting. 'A View of Royal Building for His Majesty's Horse and Foot Guards, with the Treasury in St James's Park, London.' Artist unknown. Published by T. Jeffreys, London, May 1753. *Fairhaven Collection*

Cambridge, George, Charles & the old Duke, all the staff etc following. Only towards the end, a few people below looked up as if they had found us out, but we got away easily, just as we came, & saw Albert return, loudly cheered by the crowds.[5]

The Duke of Wellington also represented the Queen at this parade, and Sir William Fraser records the following description of the last occasion upon which the Duke took part:

No military spectacle of the kind, that I have ever seen, has equalled that of the Duke's coming on to the Parade of the Flank Companies of the Foot Guards, in the rear of the Horse Guards, on the morning of the Queen's birthday. The Duke, as Commander-in-Chief, accompanied by a numerous, and most splendid Staff, rode down Constitution Hill from Apsley House. He was dressed in the uniform of his Regiment, the Grenadier Guards. The line was of course formed previous to his arrival; with the squadron of the Life Guards on duty on the right flank.

[5] RA. Queen Victoria's Journal, 27 May 1845. 'Bertie' was HRH the Prince of Wales, 'Uncle Cambridge' was Adolphus, Duke of Cambridge, tenth child and seventh son of King George III; 'George' was son of Adolphus and succeeded him as Duke. He was Commander-in-Chief of the British Army for many years. 'Charles' was the Prince of Leiningen, the Queen's half-brother, and 'the old Duke' the Duke of Wellington.

20

At the first stroke of the Horse Guards' clock, the Duke appeared on the left flank of the line. At the moment that his horse passed the extreme left, the word was given by the Commanding Officer to stand at 'Attention'; then 'Present arms'; instantly the magnificent band of the three Regiments of the Guards, with their drums and fifes, numbering together 200 instruments, played the first note of Handel's glorious air. Not since the composition of 'See the Conquering Hero comes' can it ever have been given under more effective circumstances. While listening to that grand melody you looked at the mighty conqueror.

The Duke, on arms being presented, instantly and slowly raised his right hand, nearly touching the lower right edge of his bearskin with two fingers. He rode slowly across the Parade; and the ceremony of 'Trooping the Colours' was gone through. During this time some well-chosen air, not unfrequently the 'Benediction des Poignards', from Les Huguenots, was played. The March Past followed. The united bands played Mozart's noble melody 'Non piu andrai'; the finest march for slow time that ever was composed.

Afterwards the Guards marched past in quick time; the Grenadiers playing 'The British Grenadiers'; the Coldstream Guards a beautiful March known as 'The Milanollo', the most perfect as regards time, that I have heard; the Scots Guards, the national, but mediocre melody 'Will ye

Guard Mounting, 1809. *Fairhaven Collection*

go to Inverness?' The line then advanced and presented arms; the Duke again saluted, leaving the ground amidst tumultuous cheering.[6]

Lord Rokeby, who was the first appointed Major General, had experienced great difficulty in connection with the Foot Guards' bands; so much so, in fact, that he had appealed to Prince Albert for help.

> Do you think (he wrote on 22 June 1861) I could obtain from the Prince Consort as Senior Colonel and therefore in fact commanding the Guards some authority over the bands of the three regiments so as to be able to call upon them to play *together* occasionally. At present the Lieutenant Colonels, or at least one or two of them, oppose attempts of this kind and I was obliged to write a pressing official letter to one to obtain the band of the Coldstream, the day on which the Duke of Cambridge came to the Barracks—and there was much that was arbitrarily intended in the whole proceeding. It is a great advantage for the three bands to play at times together, and as the Lieutenant Colonels would I am certain hardly ever agree to let them do so, a little power exerted by HRH the Prince Consort or delegated to me (in conjunction with the other Colonels) would be desirable. Pray consider this confidential.

But a note on this letter reads: 'HRH very unwilling to interfere with authority of Lieutenant Colonels over their respective bands . . . Thinks it better to leave them alone. June 25th.'[7]

In 1853 *Orders and Regulations for the Brigade of Guards* was published in its first edition. According to paragraph 31, 'on the Queen's Birthday the duties will be furnished by the flank companies. The Queen's Guard (with the State Colour [sic]), will be taken by the Battalion whose turn it is for the regular duties which it will mount the following day.' And paragraph 43 refers to the 'State Colour carried on the Queen's Birthday or on any other State occasion' as being lowered only to the Queen. The second edition, published in 1868, uses almost identical words, but adds that the State Colour 'will not be carried at the Birthday Parade unless Her Majesty is present'. Major Nicholas Dawnay in his book *Standards of the Household Division 1660–1973* refers to Milne's *Standards and Colours of the Army* (1890) in which Milne quotes a former Coldstream officer, General Sir Percy Fielding, 'as having said that the State Colour had been presented by Queen Charlotte and that when he joined the Regiment in 1845 it was still brought out for the Queen's Birthday Parade. Latterly, however, the Regiment had been forbidden to use it, as they could show no written authority for having it.'

It is difficult now to discover whether this reference to the State Colour really means the Queen's Colour, nor is it easy to determine how many

[6] *The History of the Scots Guards.* Sir F. Maurice, Vol. II, p. 45.
[7] RA. E. 37/74.

22

'West Front of the Horse Guards.' Coloured line engraving by H. Asland after J. Marchant, published *c.* 1845. *Fairhaven Collection*

colours were trooped. The account in the *Magazine* of 1869 refers to 'colours' in the plural, as does that for 1875, and presumably in that Journal accuracy on such a point could be expected. In the latter, however, the second Regiment of Foot Guards are called 'the Coldstreams'.[8]

At this period accounts in the *Guards Magazine* concentrated less on the military than on the social aspects of the occasion. On 2 June 1869, for example, we read that in the evening 'the club houses and theatres illuminated, as did all of the Royal tradesmen', a spectacle which defies imagination. Early in the forenoon, however, in greater sobriety, the inspection of the 'brigade of Foot Guards took place on the Parade in St James's Park'. His Highness the Nawab of Bengal and his sons, and Prince Hassan Pasha viewed the inspection from the Levee Room of the Horse Guards building which is now the Major General's Office, while the balcony of Dover House was thronged with the Princess of Wales and children, the Princess Mary Adelaide of Teck and a distinguished party.

Field Marshal HRH The Duke of Cambridge, Commander-in-Chief, arrived on the ground punctually at ten o'clock, accompanied by His Serene Highness The Prince of Teck, later the Duke of Teck, followed 'a few minutes

[8] There was issued on Saturday, 26 May 1894, an 'official Programme in honour of Her Majesty's Birthday, Trooping of the Colours by HRH The Prince of Wales', which detailed the Programme of Music both 'on the Horse Guards Parade' and subsequently at St James's Palace. Moreover, Queen Victoria constantly referred to this Regiment as 'Coldstreams', and on one occasion to the 'Scotts' Guards (RA W33/138).

after' by the Prince of Wales and the Crown Prince of Denmark. The illustrious party were received with a Royal Salute by the troops, the several bands playing 'God Save The Queen', and the Duke, accompanied by the Prince of Wales, inspected the line, after which the ceremony of 'Trooping the Colour' took place.

We know from the programme of music that on this occasion the Massed Bands and Drums of the Brigade of Guards performed the Slow Troop for the first time to the stirring tune of 'Les Huguenots', unlike 1867 when it was executed to the music of a waltz by Gounod. We also know that on this, as on all previous and subsequent parades, the Escort for the Colour (in the singular, according to the music programme) marched forward to 'The British Grenadiers', and that the Colour was trooped to 'The Grenadiers' March'. The Guards then formed open column, marched past in slow and quick time, reformed line and gave a Royal Salute. 'The Duke of Cambridge expressed himself highly pleased with the marching of the flank companies and at the soldierlike appearance of the men.' The Princess of Wales, the Princess of Teck and party remained to breakfast at Dover House.

The uniforms worn by members of the Royal Family and their relations were colourful and varied. In 1874 the Duke of Edinburgh, who had that year married the Tsar's daughter, wore that of the 2nd Uhlan Russian Light Horse, and two years later we find Prince Adolphus of Mecklenburg-Strelitz in Prussian uniform, which was hardly surprising, while the Duke of Teck was dressed in the uniform of Colonel, 1st Surrey Artillery Volunteers, which was remarkable.

In 1879 'genial weather allowed of the attendance of large numbers of people who, furnished with tickets, took up a position in the form of a square, inside of which the troops to be inspected were drawn up.' Shortly after nine o'clock 'a battalion from each regiment of Guards marched into the square, and shortly after ten o'clock the Princess of Wales with her children, the Duchess of Edinburgh and the Duchess of Teck arrived, and made their appearance at the windows of the Duke's Levee Room.' There was a degree of informality about the arrival of the military notables: about half past ten, the staff began to take up its position: Major General Stephenson, commanding the Home District (i.e. the Major General, see Appendix 4) appeared first, then came the Duke of Cambridge and Prince of Wales—the latter in the uniform of a Colonel in the Grenadier Guards. Near him rode the Crown Prince of Denmark and the Crown Prince of Sweden and Norway, the Duke of Edinburgh (this time in the uniform of an artillery volunteer officer) and the Duke of Teck; and finally, the Adjutant General, Quartermaster General and Sir Garnet Wolseley amongst 'many other general officers, military attachés and aides-de-camp whose uniforms added colour and brilliancy to the scene'. The account in the *Magazine* records that 'the colours were next given to the youngest officer present who, attended by a suitable escort, slowly and solemnly "trooped" the colours, carrying them in front of each line, the brigade being in open order formation so that every man could see his own flag as it

The Trooping on 5 June, 1875. From a woodcut by the *Illustrated London News. Fairhaven Collection*

was paraded before him, the "Grenadiers' March" being played all the while. At the completion of this ceremony, which was the principal event of the parade, the colours were saluted, and the troops marched past.'

In 1889 Queen Victoria wrote in her Journal at Windsor Castle:

24th May.
My seventieth birthday. Beatrice sent in the dear little children to wish me joy the first thing in the morning, and they sat on my bed, and were very good, Drino, with a nosegay, saying over and over again, 'Many happy returns, Gangan.' Then I got up and dressed, and went over to Beatrice, who was looking so well, and who also gave me flowers. How far away did this birthday seem from those bright happy ones from '40 to '61! Went into the Audience Room with all the others, and here the table with my presents was arranged. I received many lovely things, and endless bouquets and bunches of lilies of the valley. After eleven, we went out into the Quadrangle and sat under a canopy, facing the grand entrance, for the Trooping of the Colour, a very old ceremony. It was a beautiful sight, and one I believe I had never seen before.[9]

Two squadrons of the 1st Life Guards, with two standards and band, under

[9] The Queen had in fact watched it in 1845 (see pp. 19 and 20).

the command of Colonel Needham, were formed up on the west side of the Quadrangle, and four companies of the 2nd Battalion Grenadier Guards, under the command of Colonel Crighton-Maitland, were formed in line facing the south front. The Queen was received with a Royal Salute after which, in the words of the Court Circular, 'the usual Guard-mounting and trooping of the Queen's colour took place . . . The Troops then marched past, and reformed on their original ground, giving a Royal salute and three cheers for the Queen. Their Royal Highnesses Princess Christian, with the Princesses Victoria and Louise of Schleswig-Holstein, Princess Louise (Marchioness of Lorne), and the Duchess of Albany were present with Her Majesty. HRH Prince Henry of Battenberg was present on horseback . . . Lieutenant Colonel Lord Kilmarnock, Silver Stick in Waiting, and Colonel Wygram, the Field Officer in Brigade Waiting, were in attendance on Her Majesty.' The Field Officers and Captains of the 1st Life Guards and 2nd Battalion Grenadier Guards present at the Parade had the honour of being presented to the Queen after lunch.

Over the years the basic elements of the parade have changed little since Humphrey Bland's *Military Discipline* in his edition of 1759.[10] The origins of the part played by the Household Cavalry, however, are not so clear, but a coloured engraving by J. Maurer, *c.* 1752 (see p. 19), shows Life Guards at Guard Mounting with the Foot Guards just after the present Horse Guards Building was completed. A 1st Life Guards' Order of 27 May 1833 detailed the Household Cavalry to attend 'on the Parade Ground in front of Horse Guards tomorrow morning at ten o'clock and mount with the Guards of Infantry' (signed John MacDonald, Adjutant General). And in 1880 'a pleasant diversion was offered by a troop of The Blues which rode down the slope from the parade, its band in front, all gold and embroidery, its black horses pacing gaily, and took station to the right of the assembled bands.'

Nine years later the *Magazine* reported of the Foot Guards that 'the marching was good, although the new drill of forming, instead of wheeling, did not find so much favour with the spectators.' While the guards were furnished by the flank companies, the number varied, and in 1890, for example, there were ten; this meant that those of the 1st Battalion Grenadier Guards and 1st Coldstream had to be brought up from Pirbright 'the day before'.

Perhaps this implied that there were no rehearsals, and indeed, this shortcoming was apparent in 1892 when, because of the death of the Duke of Clarence, no members of the Royal Family were present except HRH the Commander-in-Chief. 'It was rather a hard trial for the men to march past in slow time at so short a notice, as that had been cut out from the New Drill Book, and it was not till the Monday previous that it was settled that it should be done, consequently they had little or no practice in this, the most difficult

---

[10] In *Standing Orders for the Brigade of Guards*, 1892, Appendix II (Order for the Queen's Birthday Parade), all detail of the Parade is referred to *Infantry Drill*, published by HMSO, 1889, and is almost identical to the present procedure.

marching that a soldier has to do.'[11] It is significant that the *Magazine* reports no rider to the effect that nevertheless the Commander-in-Chief was satisfied with the standard attained.

1895 was a unique year for two reasons: Birthday Parades were held on two consecutive days at Windsor and in London, and the Colours of Scots Guards battalions were trooped at each. The Queen was at Windsor for her 76th Birthday, and the entry in her diary reads:

> Windsor Castle. 24 May 1895.
> After looking at my presents, we breakfasted, & at $^{1}/_{2}$ 11 the Trooping of the Colours took place in the Quadrangle. I was present in my carriage, with Lenchen and Louise, Beatrice & Thora being in the next one. It took an hour & was a very pretty sight. The Bands played extremely well.[12]

The Court circular records the occasion: 'Her Majesty witnessed the Ceremony of Guard Mounting with Trooping the Queen's Colour in the Quad-

[11] A Coldstream Guards Order of 6 May 1768 states, '(ordered) also that in the Slow March the Men step out a smooth pace but with Spirit, gaining Ground to the Front and not raising their feet too high.'

[12] RA. Queen Victoria's Journal, 24 May 1895. 'Lenchen' was Princess Christian. She, Princess Louise and Princess Beatrice were the Queen's daughters. 'Thora' was Princess Helena Victoria, 'Lenchen's' daughter.

A Birthday Parade attended by Queen Victoria at Windsor Castle on 24 May 1895. *E. J. Collings Collection*

(*Above*) The 2nd Battalion Grenadier Guards on the Birthday Parade of Queen Victoria at Windsor Castle, 24 May 1889. (*Below*) The Escort salutes the Colour. *RHQ Grenadier Guards*

The Parade at Windsor Castle on 24 May, 1895. The Queen arrived in her carriage, accompanied by Princess Christian and Princess Louise. *E. J. Collings Collection*

rangle of the Castle. Two squadrons of the 2nd Life Guards with two standards and the Band, under the command of Lieutenant Colonel Neeld, were formed up on the West Side of the Quadrangle, and six companies of the 1st Battalion Scots Guards, under the command of Colonel Campbell, were formed up in line facing the South Front. The Queen was received by a Royal Salute. Her Majesty then drove down the line and inspected the troops, after which the usual Guard Mounting and Trooping the Queen's Colour took place.' The officers took post to the 'Garb of Old Gaul', and the Colour was trooped to 'The Grenadiers' March' and 'The Coburg March'. Colonel the Viscount Falmouth (Coldstream), the Field Officer in Brigade Waiting, was in attendance on the Queen, as was Lieutenant Colonel Sir Simon Lockhart, 1st Life Guards, the Silver Stick in Waiting, and at the end of the Parade the Queen 'expressed to the Commanding Officers Her Majesty's satisfaction at the smart appearance of the Troops and the precise execution of the several movements'.[13]

The following day, the usual parade was held in London on the Horse Guards, where the 2nd Battalion Scots Guards furnished the Escort. The occasion was covered in some detail in *The Times* of 27 May and I am indebted to the reporter of the day for these extracts from his account. The record attendance of the public was certainly not unconnected with the presence of Shahzada Nasrulla Khan, second son of the Amir of Afghanistan, who was making his first public appearance in the capital. The police, however, under Major Gilbert and Superintendent Sherlock, were present in force and 'they did not find their duties a sinecure in preventing at one or two of the more congested corners what might, but for their tact and good temper, have proved a rather serious crush.' Luckily, however, the atmospheric conditions were pleasant and genial. On Lord Falmouth of the Coldstream devolved the duty of directing the evolutions of the Troops, who in addition to the Scots Guards, were found by the 1st Grenadiers and 1st Coldstream. The Cavalry who shared in the honours of the day consisted of detachments of the 1st Life Guards and of The Royal Horse Guards (Blue), and, as usual, they made a brave show as they rode into the square. By ten o'clock, the reporter notes, all was in readiness, and 'it must have gratified Lord Falmouth to observe the splendid rigidity and military bearing of his men.'

The Levee Room was packed with Royal spectators totalling eleven, whose several arrivals by carriage were announced by fanfares of trumpets, and shortly after 10.30 the cheers swelled into a good triumphant shout as the Commander-in-Chief with the Prince of Wales, the Duke of York, the Shah-

---

[13] The Lieutenant Colonel Commanding Household Cavalry now holds the Court office of Silver Stick in Waiting and through the authority of Gold Stick Orders he details Regiments of Household Cavalry and individuals to carry out duties. He is in general charge of all duties found by the Household Cavalry for the Queen when ordered. In the past the appointment was shared by roster with the Commanding Officers of the Regiments. The Field Officer in Brigade Waiting holds an appointment in the Royal Household and is a senior officer of the Foot Guards.

zada and the Headquarters Staff arrived. Nasrulla Khan, attired in a uniform of scarlet, trimmed with gold lace and having broad fringed gold epaulettes, was attended by an interpreter and returned the greeting of the crowd by saluting in English fashion. Lord Methuen (the Major General), Sir E. Wood, Sir R. Gipps, Sir R. Buller and Sir F. Grenfell were present.

After the inspection, the Massed Bands executed the Slow and Quick Troop; 'the slow movement was particularly well done, and the manner of changing front to return at the Quick March was irreproachable.' The Right Flank Company[14] of the Scots Guards (Captain Godman) advanced to receive the colour which was trooped, and then came the word of command for the march past in column of companies, delivered in ringing tones by Lord Falmouth. 'The march past, especially in slow time, to which the troops are not accustomed, is always regarded as the crucial test on these occasions, but in this instance it was splendidly done, the most exacting of military critics finding but little opportunity for hostile comment. Occasionally there was a slight unevenness in some of the lines, but the step was perfect throughout.' Lord Falmouth led at the head of The Life Guards, followed by The Blues, the Scots, Grenadiers and Coldstream Guards. (The companies of the Coldstream were noted as being 'particularly steady in the slow movement'.) After the final Royal Salute, the Royal horsemen and Headquarters Staff were the first to leave the ground, Nasrulla Khan joining the English Princes in saluting the Royal ladies and 'realising in all its rich resonance the fullness and enthusiasm of a British Cheer'.

For many years the Salute at the Parade had been taken by HRH the Duke of Cambridge, as Commander-in-Chief. When, with great reluctance, he was persuaded at last to relinquish the appointment in 1895 the Queen, in order to soften the blow and with the agreement of her ministers, accorded to him the right of continuing to exercise this privilege. Unfortunately, however, with a change of Government no one remembered to tell either the new Secretary of State, Lord Lansdowne, or the new Commander-in-Chief, Lord Wolseley. When he heard about it, the latter said that if the Duke held the Parade in 1896 neither he nor his staff would be present. The Queen was placed in a predicament and, to get over the difficulty, decided that the Prince of Wales

---

[14] In 1831, by command of King William IV, the title of the Scots Guards was changed from 'the Third Regiment of Foot Guards' to 'Scots Fusilier Guards' and as a result the Fusiliers' system of company nomenclature was adopted as laid down in Standing Orders for the Royal Fusiliers, drawn up by HRH Prince Edward (later the Duke of Kent), Colonel of that Regiment and dated 20 October 1798: 'All officers are to understand that the terms of Right and Left Flank Company are fixed upon the application of what in other regiments of the Line are styled the Grenadier and Light Infantry Companies, it being the Colonel's pleasure that in the Royal Fusiliers it should be an esprit de Corps that the terms of Grenadier and Light Infantry should never be used ...' Despite the restoration of the original title of 'Scots Guards' by Queen Victoria in 1877, the Fusilier custom was retained in each battalion and has been ever since with the approval of another Prince Edward, Duke of Kent, who was appointed 26th Colonel in 1974.

should represent her and take the salute; on 5 May Lord Lansdowne was informed accordingly.[15]

The Duke of Cambridge decided not to attend the Parade and the matter appeared to be settled, but, on 16 May, when the Queen wrote to Lord Salisbury to tell him of the Duke's decision, she asked him to point out to Lord Wolseley 'that his action has practically obliged the Queen to revoke that which she, well within her rights, had, as Sovereign and Head of the Army, granted.'[16] On receiving the Queen's message Lord Wolseley at once wrote to Lord Lansdowne, saying how grieved he was to have incurred the Queen's displeasure and that, if she wished the Duke of Cambridge always to command the Birthday Parade in London, he would of course bow to her decision; but in that case, he asked that he and his staff should be allowed to go to Aldershot to hold the Birthday Parade there on the same day.

Lord Lansdowne forwarded the letter on to the Queen whose reaction was sharp and prompt: the same day she cyphered to Lansdowne: 'I cannot understand what Lord Wolseley means. I have deputed the Prince of Wales to hold the Parade for me and I expect the Commander-in-Chief and the Headquarters Staff to attend. The Duke of Cambridge will not be present . . . I consider the matter is now settled.'[17] At the suggestion of the Prince of Wales a communiqué to this effect was then issued to put an end to speculation in the press.[18]

On 19 May the situation was complicated yet again by the Duke of Cambridge, who sent a telegram to the Queen saying that the Prince of Wales was anxious that he *should* attend the Parade and asking what the Queen wished him to do. The Queen's somewhat ambiguous reply that she did not like to give an opinion, still less to urge him to do what he felt to be harmful[19] the Duke took to mean that she was in favour of his attending, and on the day after the Parade he wrote to her from Gloucester House:

My dear Cousin, After receipt of your telegram on Tuesday . . . I hardened my heart and made up my mind to attend, and I hope that you and others will think I did right. My own idea is now that it was better to do so, even though my personal inclination had been the other way . . .[20]

The morning of the Parade was cold, raw and wet. *The Times* report read:

The guards, which were furnished by contingents of the 3rd Grenadier Guards, the 1st and 2nd Coldstream Guards and the 1st Scots Guards stood in six companies each of 32 files, four facing east and the remainder south. On the opposite side of the square were the massed bands of the

[15] RA. W13/13, 14.
[16] RA. E40/134.
[17] RA. W13/31, 32.
[18] RA. W13/28, 36.
[19] RA. W13/40.
[20] RA. W13/42.

HM Queen Elizabeth The Queen Mother and Prince William in the Major General's office before the 1988 Birthday Parade.
Reproduced by kind permission of Lieutenant Colonel Hugh Dickens

Queen Elizabeth The Queen Mother, accompanied by the Princess of Wales, about to depart from the Horse Guards Building after the 1988 Parade. Princess Margaret and Viscount Linley can be seen walking to their car.
Photograph by the author

Two Rehearsals precede the Parade itself. Before the 1st Rehearsal in 1970, the Brigade Major, the Pipe Major of the Scots Guards, the Drum Majors, the Pipe Major of the Irish Guards and the Regimental Sergeant Major line up at Wellington Barracks. *PRO HQ London District*

The Prince of Wales, Colonel Welsh Guards, salutes the Colour as he rides past No. 6 Guard on the 2nd Rehearsal 1980 with Sylvia Stanier. *PRO HQ London District*

The Birthday Parade is watched by members of the Royal Family who drive to Horse Guards before the Queen's Procession leaves Buckingham Palace. Princess Margaret, with her children Viscount Linley and Lady Sarah Armstrong-Jones, drive to the Parade in 1974. *PRO HQ London District*

HM Queen Elizabeth the Queen Mother drives with HRH the Princess of Wales and HRH Prince William, to attend the 1987 Parade. *PRO HQ London District*

HM The Queen prepares to leave
Buckingham Palace in 1979, mounted
on her charger Burmese. She is
attended by HRH Prince Philip, Duke
of Edinburgh, Colonel Grenadier
Guards, and HRH the Prince of Wales,
Colonel Welsh Guards. *PRO HQ
London District*

Burmese, Queen's charger 1969–1986,
now retired from ceremonial duties,
with Lt Col Sir John Miller, Welsh
Guards, Crown Equerry from 1961 to
1987. *PRO HQ London District*

Brigade of Foot Guards under the command of Bandmaster and Honorary Lieutenant Dan Godfrey, the Band of The Royal Horse Guards in state uniforms, and a troop each of the 2nd Life Guards and The Royal Horse Guards . . . The Prince of Wales had been specially deputed by the Queen to represent Her Majesty at the Parade and on her behalf to take the Salute.[21] His Royal Highness was met at Marlborough House by the Commander-in-Chief and the Staff of the War Department as well as Lord Methuen and the Staff of the Home District. His Royal Highness wore the uniform of a Colonel of the Grenadier Guards and with him were the Duke of York in the uniform of the 3rd (Militia) Battalion of the Prince of Wales's Own West Yorkshire Regiment, the Duke of Cambridge, who was also in the uniform of the Grenadier Guards, Prince Christian and the Duke of Teck . . . The Commander-in-Chief wore the uniform of a Field Marshal and the sash of a Knight of the Order of St Patrick, and carried his baton.

In 1899 a new edition of *Standing Orders* cancelled that of 1892, and there it was clearly laid down that the Prince of Wales would take the Salute. At the end of the Parade HRH would leave the ground, and a separate Royal Salute would be given to any members of the Royal Family who might cross the Parade. The procedure was then similar to that of Guard Mounting from the Horse Guards today, and the Commander-in-Chief sometimes remained for this part of the ceremony.

23 May 1900 marked the last Birthday Parade of the Queen's long reign and the Colour of the 1st Battalion Grenadier Guards, wreathed in laurels for the battle honour Ramillies, was trooped. It was a singular occasion for many reasons: it was remarked that the Duke of Cambridge, for years a regular attender, was not present; one of the Queen's Colonial ADCs, thought to be General Gatacre, was dressed in khaki; the Colour was handed over to the Ensign by a Quartermaster, since Sergeant Major Fowles had been gazetted Lieutenant and Quartermaster Irish Guards that same day; and the Escort was commanded by a Captain on the Reserve of Officers (A.H.O. Lloyd).[22]

Because the War had made heavy demands upon the Household Troops, with the exception of the newly raised Irish Guards, there were only three

[21] In 1928 King George V was ill and unable to take the Salute. From his convalescence at Bognor he said that the Queen would not attend and that his uncle, HRH The Duke of Connaught, would take the Salute as Senior Colonel of the Brigade of Guards and Senior Field Marshal, *not as representative of the Crown.*

[22] During 1900 Queen Victoria's concern for her Household Troops was most marked. She inspected the 2nd Battalions of the Grenadier and Scots Guards at Buckingham Palace, the 3rd Grenadiers at Victoria Barracks, Windsor, and, also at Windsor, a draft destined to join the Grenadiers in South Africa. Barely two months before she died, when the 1st Life Guards returned from the War, arriving at Windsor Station, they at once marched to the Castle where Her Majesty was waiting in her carriage to receive them. The Queen made a speech of welcome and every officer was presented to her.

battalions of Foot Guards at home—the 1st Grenadiers, 3rd Coldstream and 3rd Battalion Scots Guards—who furnished seven guards for the Parade. The eighth was found by a unit called the Royal Guards Reserve Regiment,[23] the three officers of which were all Captains 'Late' Grenadier, Coldstream and Scots Guards. This guard was described as appearing to be 'formed of the pick of flank company men of the Brigade, all in the prime of life, and each with the Egyptian Medal and The Khedive's Star. The way they clean their buff and put on their equipment would form an instructive lesson to some of their young comrades in the Brigade . . . as to marching past (which they did to "Auld Lang Syne" and "The Boys of the Old Brigade" in slow and quick time respectively), opinion seems to give the palm to them.'[24]

The new King's reign opened with innovations to his Birthday Parade: on 24 May 1901 a parade was held on the Horse Guards in which four guards from the newly raised 3rd Scots Guards, and two each from the 1st Grenadiers, 3rd Coldstream and 1st Battalion Irish Guards took part under Colonel H. Fludyer, Lieutenant Colonel Commanding Scots Guards and Field Officer in Brigade Waiting. After inspecting the line, the King, as Colonel-in-Chief Scots Guards, handed the newly consecrated Colours to the Ensigns from his horse and they were then trooped. In the words of the Regimental Orders, there was a 'March past in slow and quick time, as usual, headed by HRH the Duke of Connaught, Colonel Commanding Scots Guards'. On the same day, the following message was published in Battalion Orders: 'Colonel Hon N. de C. Dalrymple Hamilton has it in command from HM the King to express to all members of the 3rd Battalion His Majesty's active appreciation of the manner in which the Battalion carried out the different movements comprised in today's ceremony'.[25]

The following year, the Birthday Parade again was combined with presentation of Colours, this time to the 1st Battalion Irish Guards, and it is interesting to note the arrangements for an occasion which was historic for that newly raised Regiment and indeed for the Household Troops. The Irish Guards furnished four companies (or guards in the Trooping context), the 3rd

[23] Several Reserve Regiments were formed in the infantry at this time. This Regiment comprised three companies of Grenadiers, possibly the same number of Coldstreamers and two of Scots Guards, dressed in their regimental uniforms. There was a Corps of Drums, Majors, Captains, one Lieutenant and no Ensigns. The Battalion, for that is what it was, was brigaded with the 3rd Coldstream and 3rd Scots Guards for training, went to Pirbright for musketry, was inspected by the Major General in the normal way and carried out the public duties. Colonel A. Broadwood, who had purchased his commission in the Scots Fusilier Guards in 1869, assumed command on 9 March 1900 until 15 May 1901, and the Battalion was stationed at Wellington Barracks, moving to the Tower in October 1900 where it remained until disbandment.

[24] *Household Brigade Magazine*, 1900, p. 386.

[25] *Scots Guards Magazine*, 1960, p. 60.

Grenadiers, 3rd Scots and 3rd Coldstream two each. His Majesty was dressed as Colonel-in-Chief Irish Guards, wearing the Order of St Patrick, and was greeted with a Royal Salute. He inspected the line to the music of 'Emerald Isle' and 'Killarney', and the consecration of the two new Colours then began with a rendering of 'Onward Christian Soldiers' by a 'military choir'. After the Colours had been presented by His Majesty, they were received with a general salute and marched across the parade, as is the custom today, to the National Anthem. 'At the further end of the ground,' reported *The Times*, 'the colours were placed in the hands of two Colour Sergeants, who were guarded by two tall privates,[26] the colour bearers taking up their proper places in the line.' There followed the Slow Troop by the Massed Bands ('Naturaliste') followed in quick time by 'Les Gardes de Le Reine', and then the Escort marched out to receive the Colours. These were not handed to the Ensigns by the Sergeant Major, but in other respects the procedure was in accordance with the present day. The March Past the King was headed by the Squadrons of The 1st Life Guards and Blues respectively, accompanied by the Mounted Band of The 1st Life Guards, and the Foot Guards followed in column, led by Field Marshal the Lord Roberts, Colonel Irish Guards, and Colonel Vesey Dawson, the Regimental Lieutenant Colonel. After they had passed in quick time, 'the Troops formed into line, opened ranks and gave a Royal Salute, which brought the ceremony to a close, the King riding off the ground.' The members of the Royal Family who had watched the proceedings from the Horse Guards Building then left, and 'the parade was broken up, the Guard proceeding to St James's Palace.'

That evening the King held a dinner party to mark the occasion and His Majesty's intimate association with his Army and, in particular, his Household Troops. Present were Their Royal Highnesses the Dukes of Connaught and Cambridge; Field Marshal the Lord Roberts, Commander-in-Chief and Colonel Irish Guards; Lord Wolseley (Gold Stick),[27] General Stephenson,

[26] The title of 'Guardsman' was introduced by King George V on 22 November 1918, 'as a mark of His Majesty's appreciation and pride of the splendid services rendered by the Brigade of Guards during the war'.

[27] The two Colonels of Household Cavalry hold the Court Office of Gold Stick and are 'in waiting' for alternate months. The duties of the Gold Stick are to protect the person of the Sovereign, to receive from the Sovereign orders relating to the Household Cavalry, and to pass them on for promulgation.

The appointment of Gold Stick originated as a result of a conspiracy in 1528 when King Henry VIII's life was thought to be in danger. It was therefore ordered that 'one of the Captains commanding The Life Guards should wait next to His Majesty's person before all others carrying in his hand an ebony staff with a silver head, engraved with His Majesty's cypher and crown' (Life Guards Order Book).

A note in the Royal Accounts reads, 'Monsieur St Gille Vannier to be paid his bill for a gold stick for the Captain of the Horse Guards which he carries when he waits upon His Majesty . . . £22-7-0' (Calendar of Treasury Books, Jan 1679).

King Edward, accompanied by HRH The Prince of Wales (later George V) and HRH The Duke of Connaught, arriving on Horse Guards for the 1903 Birthday Parade. At this time Number 6 Guard opened to allow the Royal procession passage to the Saluting base. *Broom Collection*

Colonel Coldstream Guards; the Quartermaster and Adjutant Generals; the Military Secretary and Chaplain General; the GOC Home District; all four Lieutenant Colonels and Silver Stick in Waiting; the Assistant Adjutant General Home District and the Brigade Major, Brigade of Guards; the Commanding Officer and Second in Command of the 1st Battalion Irish Guards, and the Field Officer in Brigade Waiting who, on this occasion, had not commanded the parade.

In 1904 the King was aboard the *Victoria and Albert* on his way to Kiel, and the Prince of Wales deputised for him, and in 1905, 1906 and 1909 rain caused cancellation.

The Parade held on 26 June 1903 was fully reported in the *Household Brigade Magazine* of that year. Assuming that the facts recorded there were accurate, there were some interesting aspects: perhaps the planners were overreacting to the importance of the occasion, but it seems like over-insurance that although the King was not timed to arrive before 11 a.m., 'the troops taking part in the Parade, and those told off to keep the ground and line the Mall, arrived shortly after 9 o'clock.' There were, apparently, two squadrons of Household Cavalry under Major A.V.H. Vaughan-Lee, Royal Horse Guards, 'distributed along the Mall' as Street Liners. (Mounted detachments were frequently deployed at street junctions on processional routes.) The King's Life Guard, a troop of The Blues and the mounted band of the 2nd Life Guards were formed up as usual on the Downing Street side, and there were ten guards under the command of the Field Officer in Brigade Waiting, Colonel Inigo Jones, Scots Guards. HRH The Duke of Cambridge was not on parade but viewed the proceedings with the Queen and the Royal ladies from the Horse Guards windows where they were joined by the Khedive of Egypt 'in the uniform of his own Army'.

The Royal procession arrived, led by Major W. Campbell, the Deputy Quartermaster General for Army Headquarters. Unlike present times, the Sovereign was *preceded* by Equerries, 'native Indian orderlies', ADCs, a mass of General Officers, members of the Army Council, Field Marshal Lord Roberts (Irish Guards), Field Marshal HRH The Duke of Connaught (Scots Guards) and the Prince of Wales in the uniform of a General. Then came the King, dressed as Colonel-in-Chief Grenadier Guards although the Colour of the 2nd Battalion Coldstream Guards was being trooped, followed by Gold Stick, the Master of the Horse and the Military Attachés, who had the honour of being presented to the King at Buckingham Palace after the Parade. The Major General (L. J. Oliphant) rode with Lieutenant General Lord Grenfell, commanding IV Army Corps, whose Chief of Staff followed with the AAG Home District, six miscellaneous full Colonels, Silver Stick in Waiting and the Lieutenant Colonels of Foot Guards, and lastly, 'lesser officers of the IVth Corps and Brigade of Guards'.[28]

Colonel Inigo Jones called the Parade from the 'slope' to the 'shoulder' to the 'present' and, without waiting for the King to arrive at the Saluting base, the National Anthem was played. The Commander-in-Chief came to His Majesty's side for the Inspection, and took station on his left on its completion with General Oliphant close behind.

After the Slow and Quick Troops by the Massed Bands to 'La Tzigane' and 'Königsgardisten', the Escort moved out to receive the Colour in *slow* time, and the March Past, with the Household Cavalry in the lead, took place as usual. At the end 'Colonel Jones calls the Parade to the Royal Salute again. The Massed Bands play the National Anthem and the King, moving forward two horses' lengths, returns the salute of his Guards. Then the King and his Staff leave the parade . . . The Queen and the rest of the Royal Family leave in open carriages a few minutes later . . . The Guard [sic] then marches to Buckingham Palace, headed by the Massed Bands . . .'

On 28 June 1907 the Irish Guards furnished the Escort, the Field Officer in Brigade Waiting was Lieutenant Colonel J. F. Erskine, Scots Guards, and the King wore the uniform of the Grenadier Guards, despite being Colonel-in-Chief Irish Guards. The Royal Procession was large and included the following: nine Royal Highnesses, Imperial Highnesses and Highnesses; three members of the Army Council; the General Officer Commanding-in-Chief

[28] A Special Army Order of 4 March 1902 announced the formation of six Army Corps Commands, into which the Districts would be merged. Thus the Home District (i.e. London District) became a part of IV Army Corps. This organisation was abolished by Special Army Order of 6 January 1905.

37

The 1908 Birthday Parade. A view of Horse Guards Parade copied from an album kept by Major A. R. Trotter (served 2nd Life Guards 1892–1920). He has pencilled a note beneath: 'Trooping the Colour 1908'. There are four Divisions of the 1st Life Guards, and their mounted band is stationed left of the massed bands. *Broom Collection*

Eastern Command, who was also Colonel Scots Guards and, except for HRH the Duke of Connaught (Grenadier Guards), the only Colonel of a Regiment of Foot Guards present; the Major General and his staff; six Equerries and four ADCs; the Gold and Silver Sticks; three Indian Orderly Officers, four Lieutenant Colonels of Foot Guards and six military attachés. If the Equerries in attendance on Members of the Royal Family in this procession are added, the total was over fifty.

For the first time it was reported in the Court Circular that 'a Royal Salute of 41 guns was fired in St James's Park by "Y" Battery Royal Horse Artillery, under the command of Major the Hon. F. R. Bingham.'

The following year, when the Colour of the 1st Battalion Coldstream Guards was trooped, the King again wore the uniform of the Grenadiers. This time His Majesty's Procession included the Chief of the General Staff and the Master of the Horse, who had not been present in 1907, and Major General Sir Stanley Clark, described as 'Clerk Marshal and Chief Equerry'. The Colonels of Foot Guards were not present, except for HRH the Duke of Connaught and the Colonel, Coldstream Guards who was the Field Officer in Brigade Waiting. It was remarked: 'One notable fact was that the French language was heard on every side, while more clergymen than is usual were present,' and that just beyond the Prime Minister's Stand 'a space was reserved for equestrians, and there must have been nearly two hundred ladies and gentlemen present on horseback.'

One of the highlights, however, must have been the presence of the Prime Minister of Nepal, His Excellency Major General Maharaja Sir Chandra Shum Shere Jung, Bahadur Rana, who rode in the procession attended by a Commanding General and another General. The Prime Minister's companions, *The Times* noticed, 'were perhaps more conspicuous in that their helmets were surmounted by flowing bird of paradise plumes.' How King Edward VII, an expert on sartorial correctness, must have enjoyed it all.

This was the last Birthday Parade attended by His Majesty in his reign. Queen Alexandra was present at them all, accompanied by other members of the Royal Family, ladies and gentlemen in attendance, and usually by a mounted Equerry. She loved a good parade, and in a letter of 27 October 1902 Lord Esher writes of an incident when a parade of Foot Guards who had served in the South African war was held on Horse Guards: 'One funny episode, *entre nous*. The King refused to let the Queen drive round, and she agreed to go up to a window with the old Duke of Cambridge. But after the King had started, she drove out of the Palace, and followed—and went all round in the procession! The old Duke in tears upstairs, at being left.'

There was no Parade in 1910 because of Court mourning, or in 1911, the year of the Coronation of King George V, but under the command of Lord Ardee, Grenadier Guards, the Field Officer in Brigade Waiting, the 1st and 3rd Battalions of the Grenadiers, the 2nd Coldstream and 1st Battalion Irish Guards moved a spectator to record of the 1912 Parade: 'Let it be Tsarskoe Selo, Potsdam or Vienna, there will be found no troops that can quite compare with the Brigade of Guards either for smartness or quick precision in drill and manoeuvre.' It is interesting to note that at this time, according to *The Times*, after the March Past and final Parade Salute, 'the New Guard fall out and take charge of the Colour. The King's Life Guard moves off and disappears into the gate of the Horse Guards; the Massed Bands and Drums of the Brigade of Guards form at the head of the New Guard and play it off to its duties at the Palace.'

The 1912 Birthday Parade, the first of King George V's reign. The mounted troops are a squadron of 1st Life Guards, and may have formed the King's Life Guard. *Broom Collection*

In 1913 Lieutenant Colonel Sir Frederick Ponsonby was Assistant Private Secretary to the King. His father, Sir Henry, had been Queen Victoria's Private Secretary for many years, and 'Fritz', as he was called, was steeped in the traditions of the Court. He became an expert on matters ceremonial, and when, at the old Queen's funeral at Windsor, the horses pulling the gun carriage which bore the coffin broke the traces, it was he who implemented the suggestion of Prince Louis of Battenberg[29] that the Naval Guard of Honour should take over, and this procedure has been followed ever since.

Before the 1913 Birthday Parade he was in correspondence with the Major General[30] and his staff about the composition of the King's procession from Buckingham Palace to Horse Guards.

The point is that the King should ride *first* down the Mall, with no one preceding him, so that the crowd down each side will be able to see him from the moment he starts. In order to make an entirely new order of march on some logical principle it will be necessary to not only consult the old records but also to decide what the Parade is, and why each individual is in the Procession.

I take it that roughly speaking the general idea is, that the Parade is held in honour of the King's Birthday, under the Command of the Field Officer in Brigade Waiting, and that His Majesty decides to be present. The King is accompanied by Princes of the Blood Royal, and attended by the Master of the Horse, Equerries, and all his Military Household. As a matter of courtesy he asks the following to accompany him and witness the Parade:

1 the Army Council
2 the Inspector General
3 the Colonels of Regiments of Guards
4 the Foreign Military Attachés
5 the GOC London District and Staff
6 the Lieutenant Colonels of the Regiments of Guards
7 the Adjutants of the Regiments of Guards.

I am not quite clear about the GOC London District but I take it that he has no status on Parade, and that he is merely an onlooker invited by the King . . .[31]

Ponsonby then retired to Kent for a few days as he was not well, but decisions had to be made quickly and the King's wishes sought as the Parade

---

[29] Father of Earl Mountbatten of Burma, sometime Colonel The Life Guards, and both 1st Sea Lords of the Admiralty.
[30] Major General Sir Alfred Codrington, Coldstream Guards, Major General 10 December 1909–2 September 1913.
[31] RA. GV Army 9875, 15 May 1913.

King George V in the Quadrangle of the Palace before or, more probably, after the 1912 Parade.
Copyright reserved. Reproduced by gracious permission of Her Majesty The Queen

would be held on 3 June. Major Clive Wigram, a fellow Assistant Private Secretary, evidently took over the responsibility at the Palace:

His Majesty approves . . .

1   the Brigade Major and a few Troopers of the Household Cavalry should ride some distance ahead but please see that they are well ahead and quite clear of the King and the Procession behind.

2   General Codrington should accompany the King when His Majesty rides round to inspect the Troops, and the Field Officer in Waiting should be the officer to receive any personal commands from the King . . .[32]

And so the arrangements for the Royal procession were executed (and the position of the Major General established) for the Parade, when the King was dressed as Colonel-in-Chief Scots Guards and was accompanied by the Duke of Connaught, Colonel Grenadier Guards, the Crown Prince of Sweden and Prince Arthur of Connaught. The Field Officer in Brigade Waiting was Lieutenant Colonel Heyworth, who became the Lieutenant Colonel Commanding in October and again commanded the 1914 Parade, some major changes for which were proposed on 4 June 1913.

General Codrington considered that improvements could be made to the proceedings at the end and suggested that the King, accompanied by his immediate entourage, should place himself between the Massed Bands and the King's Guard. 'I think the idea of the King leading his Guard away from the Parade such a good one,' he wrote, 'that although I shall not be in Command of the London District next year I mention it in order that, if His Majesty approves, it may be put on record and the question raised in due course by my successor.'[33]

Ponsonby replied, saying that the King was quite prepared to adopt the Major General's suggestion, which the Duke of Connaught also supported. He added, however, 'the only objection I personally see . . . is that there is no meaning in the King riding at the head of his own Guard. His Majesty goes to the Horse Guards Parade to see the Trooping of the Colour, and to see the Guard march off, but why the King should place himself at the head of the Guard is not quite clear.'[34] And he followed this with a suggestion of his own:

I should now like to suggest to you that His Majesty should leave the Parade at the head of all the Troops, accompanied only by the Princes of the Blood Royal, the Field Officer, and the 4 Colonels, with perhaps an Equerry added:

---

[32] *Ibid*, 19 May 1913.
[33] *Ibid*, 4 June 1913.
[34] *Ibid*, 7 June 1913.

The 1913 Trooping the Colour Ceremony. (*Below*) The duties for Guard Mounting forming up.
Broom Collection

The 1913 Birthday Parade. King George V salutes as the Household Cavalry walk past. *Broom Collection*

44

The Massed Bands
THE KING
Princes of the Blood Royal
Equerries in Waiting
4 Colonels
The Troops

On arrival at Buckingham Palace the King then might draw out and take up a position to the left of Queen Victoria's Memorial. The [New] Guard would go on straight into the forecourt, and the remainder march off to their respective Barracks. His Majesty would then ride on into the Court Yard, and be saluted by both the old and new Guard as he passed.

And he concluded on the subject of the erection of stands, to which the Office of Works were opposed: 'There would be no difficulty in filling stands even if 5/- was charged. At present the tickets given to officers' friends are a mere farce; moreover the King has no tickets at his disposal for Foreign, Indian and Colonial people of distinction.[35]

The Major General was enthusiastic but went even further and suggested that the Ground Keepers could be assembled and formed in time to join the procession down the Mall. Ponsonby, however, replied: 'if the Troops keeping the Ground were to be hurriedly assembled . . . the crowds would inevitably break in and spoil the conclusion of the Parade. From the point of view of the spectator it would be far better if the Parade Ground were left quite empty after the King and the Troops had moved off.'[36]

The King was personally involved in all the proposals and counter-proposals, and, indeed, made suggestions of his own as is evident in extracts from a letter to the Major General which Ponsonby wrote from Balmoral in September:

After the March Past is concluded, the troops to give a Royal Salute, so as to put a full stop, so to speak, on the Parade . . .

Field Officer to report to the King when all is ready, and then march off the Ground . . .

As the Guard advances, the King with the Princes, Colonels and Equerries will move out and place himself at the head of the troops . . .

The Troops keeping the Ground will remain fast until the Queen has left . . .

On arrival at Buckingham Palace the Massed Bands will take up a position outside the railings, so as to play the troops past. His Majesty is anxious that the drums should remain with the Bands . . .

The King is anxious to make a thoroughly effective conclusion to the

[35] *Ibid*, 23 August 1913.
[36] *Ibid*, 27 August 1913.

The 1914 Parade. The King rides on to the Parade Ground. *Broom Collection*

Parade, and hopes you will therefore make any further suggestions that occur to you. Next year when a rehearsal takes place it may even then be found necessary to make some alterations.[37]

Accordingly, the new Major General, Sir Francis Lloyd,[38] submitted to Major Wigram, for the King's approval, 'New arrangements for the Ceremony of Trooping the Colour', incorporating all His Majesty's proposals.[39]

The King himself read these in detail, adding further comment: 'His Majesty wishes you (one of the Major General's staff) to impress on the detachment of Household Cavalry that they should keep always quite a hundred yards ahead of the Procession. The King says they are apt to telescope up as the procession goes down the Mall.'[40] He also watched the rehearsal on 12 June from the windows of the Palace and noted some mistakes by the Foot Guards as they marched round the bend by Buckingham Palace Road.

So it was that the 1914 Parade, once again for the second year running commanded by Colonel Heyworth, incorporated many new innovations. The Queen, Queen Alexandra, Empress Marie Feodorovna of Russia and four Princesses watched from the window of the Levee Room, and the Court

[37] *Ibid*, 1 September 1913.
[38] Grenadier Guards. Major General 3 September 1913–12 September 1918.
[39] RA GV Army 9875, 13 May 1914.
[40] *Ibid*, 11 June 1914.

46

A view of the 1914 Parade. *Broom Collection*

Circular recorded for the first time: 'On the conclusion of the Ceremony, His Majesty rode back to Buckingham Palace at the head of the King's Guard, preceded by the Household Cavalry and the Combined Bands of the Brigade of Guards. On arrival at Buckingham Palace, the King's Guard entered the Forecourt and formed up opposite the Old Guard, the remaining Guards defiling past His Majesty.' 'The result of this innovation,' wrote *The Times* correspondent, 'was that a large number of the King's subjects, for whom there was no room on the Horse Guards Parade, had a close view of their Sovereign and the brilliant staff by which he was accompanied, as well as the glitter and pomp of the Massed Bands of the Foot Guards.'

This was the last Birthday Parade before the holocaust of World War I.

Following the retirement of Burmese, the Queen drove to the 1987 Birthday Parade in a phaeton first used by Queen Victoria. Here she leaves Buckingham Palace, accompanied by the Royal Colonels and her Equerries. *PRO HQ London District*

Queen Victoria in Windsor Great Park in 1845, driving in the phaeton now used by HM The Queen. Seated with her is the Marchioness of Douro, and the Duke of Wellington rides on her left. From an oil painting by Henry Barrand (1811–1874). *Duke of Wellington's collection*

The Queen's Procession arrives on Horse Guards Parade. Following Her Majesty (*below*), behind the Royal Colonels and Equerries, ride (*left to right*) General Sir Desmond Fitzpatrick, Colonel The Blues and Royals; Major General Sir George Burns, Colonel Coldstream Guards; Major General Christopher Airy, the Major General. 1987 Parade. *PRO HQ London District*

HM The Queen at the Saluting base in front of the Horse Guards Building. In 1968 (*above*) the day had begun with heavy rain, but had cleared in time for the Parade. At the 1974 Parade (*below*) the Queen on Burmese stands accompanied by HRH the Duke of Edinburgh, Colonel Welsh Guards, and HRH the Duke of Kent, Personal Aide-de-Camp to Her Majesty and wearing the full dress uniform of the Royal Scots Dragoon Guards. *PRO HQ London District*

During the Quick Troop, one side drummer leaves the Massed Bands and moves to the right of the Escort for the Colour, ready to sound the 'Drummer's Call'. *PRO HQ London District*

The Massed Bands are halted in front of the Guards, with the Household Cavalry behind them. *PRO HQ London District*

1919 to 1939

In 1919 the Guards Division came home from Germany, and on 3 June of that year the Birthday Parade was held for the first time since 1914. Horse Guards Parade could not be used because huts had been erected there, and so on the 54th anniversary of the King's birthday it took place in Hyde Park. His Majesty wrote in his diary: 'at 10.30 I rode to the Guard Mounting in Hyde Park, it was a beautiful sight and the troops did it better even than before the war.'[1]

It was, in fact, the largest Birthday Parade to be held before or since: 1st and 2nd Life Guards, and The Blues each furnished two troops totalling 9 officers and 213, with three bands of 1 and 89, while the Foot Guards found eleven Guards, including one from the Guards Machine Gun Regiment, and 473 Musicians, Drummers and Pipers. 1st and 2nd Guards Brigades[2] provided the Ground Keepers; the King's Colour of the 3rd Coldstream was trooped, and the Regimental Lieutenant Colonel of the Irish Guards was the Field Officer in Brigade Waiting.

The Royal procession from Buckingham Palace was led by a staff officer of HQ London District, and following the King were the Prince of Wales, the Duke of Connaught (Colonel, Grenadier Guards), Prince Arthur of Connaught, the Marquess of Cambridge and the Earl of Athlone. Next came Gold Stick in Waiting and the Equerries to the King, the Army Council and 'Field Marshal Commanding-in-Chief, Great Britain', fourteen Military Attachés, two ADCs to the King, the staff of the Field Marshal, and the Guards Brigade Commanders.[3] The Major General was accompanied by a staff of five, and the Guards Brigade Brigade Majors rode with them. Colonel Trotter of the Machine Gun Regiment and Captain Curtis, his Regimental Adjutant, were also

---

[1] RA. King George V Diary. 3 June 1919.

[2] A Special Brigade order, published from Headquarters 1st Guards Brigade, 'Horse Guards Annexe, Carlton House Terrace', survives.

[3] Brigadier General the Master of Ruthven, 1st Brigade, and Brigadier General Matheson, the 2nd Brigade, who had previously commanded, as a Major General, the Guards Division.

49

The 1919 Birthday Parade in Hyde Park. Nearest the camera is Edward, Prince of Wales. *E. J. Collings Collection*

there. The whole of this procession, totalling 73, accompanied the King when he inspected the troops who, with the exception of the Drum Majors and musicians, wore Service Dress.

The Field Officer led the March Past, riding ten paces in front of the Household Cavalry, and it was the Major of the Parade who ordered the Foot Guards to break into quick time. At the end of the Parade, in the words of the order from 'The London District Office' in Carlton House Terrace:

His Majesty has signified his intention of riding as far as Hyde Park Corner between the Massed Bands of the Household Cavalry and the leading sections of the Household Cavalry; after the Household Cavalry has marched past, His Majesty the King will ride to Buckingham Palace between the Massed Bands of the Brigade of Guards and the King's Guard. His Majesty will be accompanied by HRH The Prince of Wales, HRH The Duke of Connaught, attended by the Equerry-in-Waiting, the two Colonels of the Regiments of Foot Guards and the Field Officer in Brigade Waiting.

The next year, 1920, found, presumably, the huts still barring the Horse Guards Parade because Hyde Park was again used. A Special Correspondent of *The Times* described the event:

50

The Colour of the 3rd Coldstream Guards being trooped at the 1919 Parade. The Colour is carried by Second Lieutenant G. Watkins. *Broom Collection*

It was bitterly cold. The waiting troops, of whom some 1,770[4] were on parade, could be seen blowing on hands and stamping feet. It was with general relief that the arrival of the Queen and Princess Mary, a few minutes before 11 o'clock, gave an opportunity for brisk movements of rifle and allowed loyal and chilled subjects to stand up (without being ordered to sit down by ruthless subalterns) and stamp surreptitiously.

The Duke of York was noted as 'looking very boyish in the very latest airforce blue' and 'the Military Attachés of Foreign powers lent a splash of colour to the procession which again reverted to type in the shape of red tabs and gilt hats'.

When the Royal Standard was broken at the pavilion, the Special Correspondent reported that the troops presented arms rather raggedly because Colonel Cator, Scots Guards, had to shout against a strong wind. 'The Salute acknowledged, the procession trooped round,' went on this humourist, 'to ascertain if the men were really there, and the massed bands, under Captain A. Williams, proceeded to give a lively rendering of one of its conductor's compositions.'

As was customary, the Household Cavalry preceded the Foot Guards in the

---

[4] Compared with 2,199 in 1919.

Senior officers of the Foot Guards at the 1920 Parade held in Hyde Park. *Broom Collection*

March Past, and the procedure at Hyde Park Corner and in the march to the Palace was the same as in 1919.

Last year, however, the troops taking part in the ceremony were for the most part war-tried veterans. This year there were many young soldiers, though here and there gleamed medals and the officers made a good show. Their steadiness was worthy of the best traditions of the Brigade, and it was noted by all with approval that the two regiments marked down for destruction were as smart as any on parade, and there was more than one challenging glance made by old Irish and Welsh Guards officers at the figure of the Secretary of State for War, as he stood with his little girl behind the Sovereign, watching proceedings a little gloomily.'[5]

[5] Winston Churchill was the Secretary of State, and this refers to a proposal which was under discussion in the War Office, whereby the Irish Guards would be in some way amalgamated with the Scots Guards, and the Welsh Guards reduced to the strength of a single company and become a part of the Grenadier Guards. In the event, this scheme was, of course, abandoned. Nevertheless, in his memoirs Oliver Lyttelton (Lord Chandos) recalled, '. . . after the War Winston used to thunder, "Star, Thistle and Grenade! They should be the only Guardsmen."'

52

King George V takes the Salute at the 1920 parade. To the right of the picture is Mr Winston Churchill, the Secretary of State for War, with his daughter. *Illustrated London News Picture Library*

This was the first appearance on a Birthday Parade of the pipers of the Irish Guards. They did not exist before the War, and the first two sets of Irish pipes were presented to the Regiment by John Redmond MP, a Home Rule leader whose son was serving with them as an officer, and awarded the DSO. After the War the unofficial pipes were given recognition but were not established.

(The Regimental Wolfhound, the first of whom was presented by the Irish Kennel Club on 15 October 1902, and joined the 1st Battalion at the Tower of London, has never taken part in the Parade but marches in front of the Band which leads the Guards, furnished by the Regiment, to Horse Guards. He then falls out.)

In 1921 the Parade, for the first time since 1914, was held on the Horse Guards and in full dress, and spectators saw two troops of the Household Cavalry (on this occasion from the 2nd Life Guards) and the Mounted Band formed up on the South side by the Downing Street wall, and eight Guards, formed by the 1st and 3rd Battalions Grenadiers, 1st Coldstream, and 1st and 2nd Battalions Scots Guards, in their usual places. The Household Cavalry walked and trotted past the King, before His Majesty placed himself at the head of the New Guard for the ride down the Mall to the Palace.

The Prince of Wales, who had been appointed Colonel of the Welsh Guards

53

The Foreign Attachés salute the King as he leaves Buckingham Palace for the 1921 Parade on Horse Guards. *Broom Collection*

The Foreign Attachés arrive on the Parade Ground. *Broom Collection*

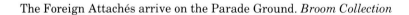

The 1921 Birthday Parade. *Broom Collection*

on 3 June 1919, was on parade. He tells the following story:

> Having accoutred myself with considerable care at York House, I mounted my horse and rode over to Clarence House to fetch my great-uncle (HRH The Duke of Connaught, Colonel Grenadier Guards) and accompany him to Buckingham Palace to join the King's procession to the Horse Guards. He was waiting for me on the steps. As I saluted, his eagle eye darted over my uniform to rest finally for interminable seconds at my waist. 'My dear boy,' he said coldly, 'don't you realise that you are improperly dressed? You are in "guard order" when you should be in "review order".' The first prescribed a crimson silk sash and white leather sword slings and knot; the other, a gold and crimson net sash and gold lace sword slings and knot. I turned my horse around and trotted shamefacedly back to York House, where, without my dismounting, the correct accoutrements were girt around me. The idea of having thus saved me from so embarrassing a military error evidently gave him satisfaction. At every Birthday Parade thereafter he never failed to remind me of the incident. 'Do you remember that day when you started for parade in the wrong order? Wasn't it lucky I spotted it in time?'[6]

[6] *A King's Story*. HRH The Duke of Windsor. Cassell, 1951, p. 190.

55

The 1921 Parade. HM King George V, dressed as Colonel-in-Chief Grenadier Guards, attended by HRH The Prince of Wales, Colonel Welsh Guards, and HRH the Duke of Connaught, Colonel Grenadier Guards. *Broom Collection*

The Prince of Wales became Colonel-in-Chief of all the Regiments of Household Cavalry and Foot Guards on his succession to the throne, but he retained the Colonelcy of the Welsh Guards; this was unique.[7] He relinquished all his appointments with the Household Troops on his abdication. As Duke of Windsor he wore Welsh Guards Service Dress during the War, with the badges of rank of a Major General, and maintained a great affection for the Regiment, the first Battalion of which he visited in Germany in 1951. He remained, until his death, Patron of the Prince of Wales Company Club, and to this day at the annual dinner a toast is drunk to him as 'the Founder'.

[7] It might not have been. Speaking at a Scots Guards Association dinner in Dundee on 11 December 1936, Lord Glamis, the eldest brother of the new Queen (the present Queen Mother) said, 'Considering the extremely difficult position in which the new King has been placed for the last few weeks', a message should be sent saying that members of the Branch hoped that he would remain Colonel of the Regiment.

King George V and Marshal Foch in the Palace Quadrangle before the 1925 Birthday Parade.
The Marshal is wearing the riband and star of the Order of the Bath, of which he was a Knight
Grand Cross. *Archives Nationales, Paris*

Major General Sir George Jeffreys, who started an article in the 1924
Autumn number of the *Magazine* with the words, 'I am asked by the Editor to
write a few notes about the Trooping of the Colour on the occasion of His
Majesty's Birthday this year', recorded his observations with an experienced
and critical eye:

The two sentries on the Colour were particularly good, moving and
handling their arms perfectly together and with absolute precision . . .
The Troop by the Massed Bands was as impressive as ever . . . The Escort
for the Colour under Lieutenant P. Ellison was very good, and the Ensign
(2nd Lieutenant R. R. A. Smith) struck me as being particularly smart in
his movements and handling of the Colour. It may be here remarked in
passing that many old friends of the late Lieutenant Colonel Wilfred
Smith were delighted to see that gallant officer's son carrying the Colour
of the Battalion at the head of which his father died in the Great War . . .
The March Past of the Foot Guards in slow time struck me as good; that

The King, with Marshal Foch, arrives on Horse Guards Parade (*above, Archives, Nationales, Paris*)

Arthur, Duke of Connaught, taking the Salute outside Buckingham Palace at a rehearsal of Trooping the Colour, 1928. *Copyright reserved. Reproduced by gracious permission of Her Majesty The Queen*

58

in quick time as less good . . . The steadiness and handling of arms were good throughout the ceremony and it is permissible to remark that in the Field Officer in Brigade Waiting (Colonel J. V. Campbell, vc, Coldstream Guards), the parade had a commander whose soldierly figure was in keeping with the traditions of the occasion.

On 2 June the following year Marshal Foch, who was not only a Marshal of France but also a British Field Marshal, arrived in London at the King's invitation. The next day there can have been no prouder man riding with the Military Attachés on the Trooping than General Vicomte de la Panouse, the French representative, when he saw his Marshal, wearing the riband of the Grand Cross of the Order of the Bath and accompanied by his ADC, on parade. After the Inspection HRH The Duke of Connaught and he took up position on either side of the King and later rode down the Mall with His Majesty.

There was no Parade in 1926 because of the General Strike, and 1928[8] saw the Colour of the 1st Battalion Welsh Guards trooped for the first time, with the Regimental Lieutenant Colonel (Colonel T. R. C. Price) as the Field Officer. The King was not well during the next two years and the Duke of Connaught, as Senior Colonel, took the Salute in 1929 and should have done so in 1930 but was advised by his doctors not to, and so watched the Parade from the Horse Guards windows while the Prince of Wales deputised. A microphone hung in front of the Horse Guards Archway and a gramophone recording of the ceremony was made. There was also a broadcast commentary by the BBC, and for the first and last time, in addition to the Military Attachés of foreign powers, military representatives of Canada, Australia, New Zealand and South Africa were present. But the following year saw the King back on parade, and it was noticed that there were three holders of the VC in the Royal procession: General Sir Alexander Cobbe, ADC General, Colonel J. V. Campbell, ADC to the King, and Colonel Viscount Gort, Lieutenant Colonel Grenadier Guards.

Four days after the Parade, Mr Kirkwood (Dumbarton Burghs, Lab.) rose in the House of Commons and asked whether, as this was an age of economy, this ceremony of Trooping the Colour could not be dispensed with 'as it was bound to cost a lot of bawbees' (laughter). No answer was given.

In 1932 the Parade nearly saw the recruitment of a distinguished Royal

---

[8] In February 1928 the pipers of the Scots Guards were authorised to wear feather bonnets in place of glengarries which had been worn previously. Before 1856 there were no pipers on the regimental Establishment, although some Company Commanders provided themselves with them unofficially. In 1853 a pipe major was appointed, again unofficially, by the 1st Battalion during the Crimea War, but three years later a Pipe Major and five pipers, seconded from the Black Watch, were approved. King George V personally decided the details of the bonnet and hackle which he commanded should replace the glengarry in 1928, and indeed offered to pay the total cost. (RA. GV Army Dress Regulations 47491.)

King George V and his sons returning from the Parade of 4 June, 1928, watched by Queen Mary and the Royal Party. The figure saluting by the archway is a King's Marshalman, of whom there were six. They did duty as police at the Palace and the Houses of Parliament up to 1939, but were not re-established after the war. *Copyright reserved. Reproduced by gracious permission of Her Majesty The Queen*

Cavalryman to the 'Empty Saddle Club'.[9] HRH The Duke of Gloucester, in the uniform of his old Regiment, the 10th Hussars, was paired in the Royal procession with Lord Athlone. A spectator recorded:

> While the procession was returning to the Saluting base, the Duke's charger entered a rather active protest against the noise made by the bands and the fact that it was expected to wear a crupper to which it was

[9] A club composed of those officers (exclusively Foot Guards but distinguished) who have had the misfortune to dismount involuntarily. Some who did not technically qualify had singular experiences: In the Scots Guards alone an Adjutant in Brigade Waiting, who subsequently became the Major General, returned his sword into his charger's rump, with dire consequences; a famous tableau of 'Scotland the Brave', when the Major of the Parade's horse took exception to the Drummer's Call, and took off on a *pas gymnastique* for the Horse Guards Arch where he caused chaos; and a battalion adjutant in the Mall who, according to one account, went backwards from the Palace to Admiralty Arch and, to another, bolted in the reverse direction with his sword between his teeth, full tilt into the 1st Division of the Escort.

60

not accustomed. It kicked out in a way that was not merely a severe test of its rider's horsemanship but induced his neighbours to give the animal a wide berth. The Duke soon reduced it to order, but it was not surprising that after the procession had formed up before the Horse Guards Arch he left the parade for a short space, to reappear later on a better behaved mount.

HRH The Duke of York succeeded to the Colonelcy of the Scots Guards on the death of Lord Methuen and was on parade in the uniform of the Regiment (as opposed to that of the Royal Air Force) in 1933, when, one would have thought improbably, an observer of the Parade noted in the stands that 'here and there the white drill uniform and sun helmet of an officer on leave from the East excited the envy of the men in conventional mufti'. But it *was* extremely hot, in contrast to 1934 when the King, at the opening of his 70th year, was well enough to take the Salute on a bitterly cold, grey day. The King of Siam watched, but one gets an impression of unusual gloom. *The Times* commented, 'Had the white ensigns and other flags hanging from the windows of the Admiralty been clean, they would have done much to lighten the outlook.' Second Lieutenant H. N. Clowes carried the King's Colour of the

The Household Cavalry walk past during the Parade on 4 June, 1932. Members of the Army Council and military attachés, mounted, are in the foreground. *Copyright reserved. Reproduced by gracious permission of Her Majesty The Queen*

The Colonels of Foot Guards Regiments in 1933. Left to right: the Duke of York (Scots Guards), Lord Cavan (Irish Guards), the Prince of Wales (Welsh Guards), the Duke of Connaught (Grenadier Guards) and Sir Alfred Codrington (Coldstream Guards). *Copyright reserved.* *Reproduced by gracious permission of Her Majesty The Queen*

1st Battalion Scots Guards and in 1973 was appointed Standard Bearer of the Honourable Corps of Gentlemen-at-Arms, so it can be assumed that he carried out his duties in an exemplary manner in his youth, although he recalls that 'my right arm went completely to sleep after the Troop, and when we turned about to face the Guards Memorial I changed arms and held the Colour for a few minutes with my left hand. I was terrified that some one or camera would spot it but I got away with it and never dared to admit it till now (1978). I wonder if anyone else has ever done it? Too risky with TV, but better than dropping it.'

King George V took the Salute for the last time in 1935, and he was attended by all his sons. This had not happened before: the Prince of Wales was in the uniform of the Welsh Guards, the Duke of York that of the Scots Guards, while Prince Henry wore again his old Regimental uniform and the Duke of Kent that of the Queen's Own Royal West Kents. The King was also attended by Major General The Maharajah of Jammu and Kashmir, Lieutenant General The Maharajah of Bikaner and Nawab Malik Sir Umar Hayad

Queen Mary, the Duchess of York, Princess Elizabeth, Princess Margaret and the Duchess of Kent attend King George V's last Birthday Parade, 3 June, 1935. *Copyright reserved. Reproduced by gracious permission of Her Majesty The Queen*

Khan, all His Majesty's Honorary ADCs. It was a truly memorable occasion.

Colonel Sir Arthur Erskine no doubt remembered it for other reasons. He was the Crown Equerry from 1924 to 1941, and it was during this period that he is recorded as having made the following pungent comments about certain aspects of the Parade:

None of the Princes or Staff saluted when 'God save the King' was played after the Ensign had taken over the Colour from the Regimental Sergeant Major. This should be rectified next year.

It would be better another year if it was explained to the Princes and Colonels of Regiments that they should turn into the Forecourt on return to the Palace through the South Gate after passing His Majesty, and not through the Centre Gate. This will make it easier for them to form up behind the King.

Make sure that the Brigade Major understands that the King goes his own pace down the Mall and that the Brigade Major must keep his proper

The King, Colonel-in-Chief Irish Guards, leaves Horse Guards with the Field Officer in Brigade Waiting, for the last time. *Copyright reserved. Reproduced by gracious permission of Her Majesty The Queen*

64

TRH The Dukes of York, Gloucester and Kent arrive on Horse Guards for the 1936 Birthday Parade. *The Photo Source/Keystone*

King Edward VIII taking the salute at the Palace after the only Birthday Parade of his reign, 23 June, 1936. *PRO HQ London District*

distance from the King and not expect the King to keep his distance from the Brigade Major.[10]

On 23 June 1936 King Edward VIII held the only Birthday Parade of his short reign, and his cypher stood out vividly on the State dress of the Household Cavalry Musicians and Drum Majors of the Foot Guards. The King's Colour of the 1st Battalion Grenadier Guards was trooped, and *The Times* correspondent noticed some innovations in dress and drill. The Riband of the Order of the Garter was not worn by the King or royal princes: 'Such ribands of orders are not to be worn in future in [sic] outdoor parades.' 'The Mounted Officers of the Guards,' he wrote, 'have now discarded again their knee-high riding boots for the red striped overall which was the Trouser worn the last time these full dress uniforms were seen in actual war, in the Crimea, and the changed form of the officers' salute, carrying the down pointed sword to the side, reverts to the seventeenth century, though no hats are now raised.'[11]

It is quite possible that the King, who favoured new ideas, might well have introduced into this Parade two further innovations which were seen the following month in Hyde Park when new colours were presented to six battalions: Firstly, when His Majesty inspected the Line, the Standard of The Blues who furnished the Escort was borne behind him as he did so, only rejoining the Escort on completion of the Inspection; and secondly, the Drummer's Call was beaten by the Massed Drums. Both were reported by Major General Sir George Jeffreys as 'extremely effective'.

Before the advent of television, which has enabled millions worldwide to watch the Sovereign's Birthday Parade and to see more aspects than are visible to participants and spectators on the ground, newspaper coverage was considerable. In *The Times* of 24 June 1936, to take but one example, naturally there was the Court Circular. In addition, there was a quarter

---

[10] The author recalls that these comments referred to a single Birthday Parade but the date of the memo and to whom it was addressed are not known. George Stone, Irish Guards and formerly Garrison Sergeant Major, recalls that the Derby Dinner was usually held on the evening of the Birthday Parade. 'The then Pipe Major of the Irish Guards (Thomas Atkins) told me the King said to him after the Dinner, "My old horse likes to get up among the pipers (on the ride back to the Palace), especially during the playing of 'The Wearing of the Green'."'

[11] 1936 saw several other changes, as recorded by Lt. Col. (later Brigadier) A. H. C. Swinton, father of Major General Sir John Swinton, later the Major General, in the 1938 volume of the *Journal* of the Society of Army Historical Research. 'In order,' as he put it, 'that future generations may be spared the labour of research among orders that are not easy of access, I append some notes on various changes that have taken place in the Brigade of Guards recently.' (His foresight was prophetic as all the archives of the Brigade Office were destroyed by water while they lay in the cellars of the Horse Guards building during World War II.) He noted that on 21 July 1936 it was decided to abolish the folded greatcoat and to experiment with a folded cape. A Brigade Order of 13 October that year stated: 'Folded capes, 14 inches by 6½ inches, with three folds and with ornaments to be worn on the back, the top of the cape to be in line with the piping on the top of the tunic collar.'

column on the main news page, nearly one and a half columns in the 'Home News', and a Fourth Leader in which the writer excelled himself:

> By a happy accident of nativity, King Edward's birthday, falling between the solstice and Midsummer day, takes rank in the calendar, as a King's birthday should, at the very height and crown of the Season. Yesterday the glory of the sunshine was worthy of the splendour of the traditional scene, and consummated the first official military pomp of the new reign.
>
> This lordly ceremonial is an archaism that has never become an anachronism. With the utmost splendour of scarlet and gold, with drawn swords and fixed bayonets, and drums, bugles for defiance, the Guards proclaim their readiness to defend the King's person—which is in no danger. But the King's person is the symbol of the past and future of his people . . . The watching multitudes know that the Salute of the Guards to the King is a salute that they themselves share in and themselves receive; for King and Army and People are one in a trinity on whose maintenance depends the nation's life and freedom . . . They draw inspiration from the matchless martial dignity and discipline of these picked men of the professional Army who will be the first bulwark of defence if attack should come, and whose pride is to keep the valiant succession unbroken through the quiet years.

It is customary for the Queen, as wife of the Sovereign, to invite her guests to watch the Parade from the windows of the Major General's Office. Today this is done by Queen Elizabeth The Queen Mother, but in 1936 King Edward VIII's Private Secretary, Major Alexander Hardinge, wrote to Queen Mary's Lady in Waiting: 'The King told me to find out what the Queen's wishes are with regard to being present at the Birthday Parade.' Her Majesty wrote on this note, 'I will think this over but I hope anyhow that the other members of the family will be present, those who have always been hitherto.'[12] The King provided seats for his future wife and a friend in a stand.

King George VI, who as Duke of York had been Colonel Scots Guards[13] and on his accession became Colonel-in-Chief of the Regiments of Household Cavalry and Foot Guards, approved some significant alterations to the procedure for the first Birthday Parade of his reign. These were promulgated in an Instruction dated 19 March 1937 (3000/BM) over the signature of the Brigade Major, extracts from which are as follows:

> Instead of the two troops and band of the Household Cavalry parading with the Foot Guards on the Horse Guards Parade, a Sovereign's Escort from the Regiment quartered in London will accompany His Majesty

[12] RA. GVI PS39/TR, 25 May 1936.

[13] He was succeeded as Colonel by HRH the Duke of Gloucester who till his death wore his father's bearskin cap. This was passed on in 1974 to the 26th Colonel, HRH the Duke of Kent, and so is about 80 years old.

from Buckingham Palace to the Horse Guards Parade: the two rear divisions of the Escort marching in rear of the normal Royal Procession.

On reaching the Parade Ground the first and second divisions of the Escort will lead His Majesty on to the Parade and continue on past the Saluting Base: they will halt facing Downing Street directly His Majesty reaches the Saluting Base and remain there while His Majesty receives the Royal Salute.

The Instruction then stated that while the King inspected the Foot Guards, the first and second divisions of the Escort countermarched and formed up by sections facing north, with the third and fourth divisions on their left. When the King had completed his inspection and returned to the Saluting base, the Field Officer called the Guards to attention and the Escort marched past His Majesty by sections at the walk, returning to barracks. And the Instruction ended: 'When the rear of the Escort is clear of the left flank of the left Guard, the Field Officer in Brigade Waiting will give the command "Troop".'

The year 1938 witnessed the last appearance in the Royal procession of the Military Attachés and Military Members of the Army Council. The Chief of the Imperial General Staff, Adjutant and Quartermaster Generals had been

Queen Mary, with Princess Elizabeth and Princess Margaret, arrives on Horse Guards Parade for the 1938 Parade. *Copyright reserved. Reproduced by gracious permission of Her Majesty The Queen*

Queen Mary, with the Duchess of Kent, Prince Edward and Princess Alexandra, and Mary, Princess Royal, Countess of Harewood (right), on the balcony of the Palace after the Birthday Parade on 8 June, 1939. *Copyright reserved. Reproduced by gracious permission of Her Majesty The Queen*

regular attenders, together with the Master General of the Ordnance, who for this year had been displaced by the Director General of the Territorial Army, and on two fleeting occasions by an 'Inspector General'. It was also of importance because the King agreed to the BBC televising the proceedings 'as an Experiment and not as a permanent concession.' Queen Mary, accompanied by Princess Elizabeth and Princess Margaret, drove to Horse Guards Parade in a carriage with a Captain's Escort of The Life Guards with Standard. This had not been seen before.

The last Birthday Parade before the Second World War was held on 8 June 1939.[14] The King was in North America but decided that the Parade would not be postponed until after his return. His Majesty ordered that the Salute would be taken by HRH the Duke of Gloucester, accompanied by the Duke of Kent and the Earls of Harewood and Athlone. Prince Henry would have a Captain's Escort, one Household Cavalry Band would be present, but no members of the Army Council nor the Master of the Horse, Gold and Silver Sticks in Waiting. The King also wished HRH the Duchess of Gloucester to invite Members of

[14] On 27 July the Rt. Hon. Herwald Ramsbotham, HM Office of Works, wrote a Secret memorandum to the King's Private Secretary warning that because shelters might have to be built beneath Horse Guards Parade, the 1940 Trooping and rehearsals might have to be held elsewhere, and Hyde Park was suggested as an alternative. This project, however, was cancelled. RA. GVI PS39/TR.

70

the Royal Family to watch, and amongst those in the Major General's room were Princess Barbara of Prussia, the Crown Princess of Sweden, Queen Victoria Eugenie of Spain and the Infanta Maria Christina. Queen Mary attended with Princess Elizabeth and Princess Margaret Rose who travelled by carriage, without Escort.

The Regimental Lieutenant Colonel Welsh Guards was the Field Officer in Brigade Waiting, and as there were only three Battalions in the 'West End' [sic], the Major General obtained the King's permission that only six Guards should be furnished—the Escort and No. 2 Guard by the 2nd Grenadiers, Nos. 3 and 4 by the 1st Coldstream and the remainder by the 1st Battalion Irish Guards. This was despite the deployment of four officers and 160 ground keepers and 20 Officers and 530 street liners. The Band of the Coldstream Guards was at the British Pavilion at the New York World Fair and therefore was not on parade. The Pipes and Drums of the 1st Battalion Scots Guards were, however, present, and for the last time two Indian Orderly Officers to the King were in the procession.

Although the King was not present with his Guards in London, while he was in Canada the Canadian Guards performed the Ceremony of Trooping in the presence of His Majesty in Ottawa. *The Times* comments: 'That occasion was unique in the annals of Empire and adds a happy note to the traditional alliance of those Coldstream and Grenadier Guards who were on parade in London yesterday with the Governor General's Foot Guards of Ottawa and the Canadian Grenadier Guards of Montreal.'

1947 to 1988

The first Birthday Parade after World War II was held on Thursday 12 June 1947. A stir was caused in certain Foot Guards circles because the King's Colour of the 2nd Battalion Coldstream Guards was trooped and Lieutenant Colonel the Viscount Dalrymple, Commanding the 2nd Battalion Scots Guards, was the Field Officer in Brigade Waiting. As we have seen, however, historically there had never been any custom whereby the Field Officer for the month automatically came from the Regiment whose Colour was trooped, and indeed the Parade of 1939 was commanded by the Regimental Lieutenant Colonel Welsh Guards and the Escort found by the 2nd Grenadiers.[1]

All ranks wore battledress except for the Sovereign's Escort of the Household Cavalry, mounted officers, and members of the Regimental Bands who were in Service Dress. HRH The Princess Elizabeth had been appointed Colonel Grenadier Guards in 1942. She rode side saddle and was in blue uniform, wearing a forage cap which later became in style that of the WRAC.

The Times reported: 'Since the last King's Birthday Parade, the Guards have been far afield and have had little time for ceremonial; but yesterday they showed they had lost nothing of their incomparable steadiness on parade. Even in battledress with the unimpressive modern rifle and bayonet these Guards continue to be supremely soldier like.' The Sovereign's Escort of seven Officers and 109 took up position in front of the Guards Memorial. In the words of the Orders: 'After the Royal Salute, His Majesty . . . will proceed to inspect the Line and the Household Cavalry Escort . . . When the Massed Bands of the Brigade of Guards commence the Slow Troop, the Household Cavalry Escort will move off Parade and return to Hyde Park Barracks.'

---

[1] Even more specifically, Guards Division Order No. 2 of 18 May 1857 laid down that 'the Field Officer and Adjutant for the Horse Guards Parade (Trooping the Colours) are to be furnished by the Battalion which finds the Queen's Guard, except on the Queen's Birthday Parade.' With effect from 1987 the Commanding Officer of the Battalion finding the Escort is the Field Officer in Brigade Waiting for that occasion only. At all other times the 'Colonel Foot Guards' is permanently in waiting.

72

The first appearance of Princess Elizabeth on horseback at an official ceremony: HRH, with HM King George VI, arriving on Horse Guards for the Birthday Parade on 12 June, 1947.
Illustrated London News Picture Library

73

In the order of March to Buckingham Palace after the ceremony on Horse Guards Parade, in the words of Household Division Standing Orders, 'the Procession is closed by the Brigade Major' who follows the other Mounted officers who do not immediately follow the Sovereign.

Major W. A. G. Burns, Coldstream Guards, later the Major General, Colonel of the Regiment and a Steward of the Jockey Club, filled that appointment in 1947. He recalls that after he had ridden past and saluted His Majesty and was about to turn through the South Centre Gate into the Palace Forecourt, his charger was frightened by the Massed Foot Guards Bands. 'It shied, skidded and eventually ended up on the pavement where it came down with all four legs under it, thus causing me to quit the saddle and lose my forage cap.' This incident, not at that time recorded on television but viewed by Queen Elizabeth from the balcony of the Palace, was also marked by the prints of his horse's hooves on the pavement which were visible for the rest of the year.

This was also the first Birthday Parade under Major General John Marriott, Scots Guards, as the Major General.

In the New Year (he wrote in the *Scots Guards Magazine* of 1962) I submitted a letter to the War Office on the reintroduction of full dress for the Brigade of Guards . . . The Secretary of State for War, the Rt. Hon. Emmanuel Shinwell, sent for me. I didn't know him at all well but I had the highest regard for 'Mannie'. He was a great enthusiast for the Army, to the point, and to my mind, absolutely genuine. To my astonishment and immense pleasure, he agreed. 'How soon can you do it?' he said. 'Not before the Trooping,' I replied. 'Can't you put something on before that?' 'Yes,' I answered, 'I can put on a massed band parade on the Horse Guards.' 'Excellent, do that,' said Mannie . . . The King was a little dubious about returning to full dress. 'I think,' he said, 'that you are going a bit too fast. Let us get into "Blue" first.' I knew that was fatal, but I also knew I had his blessing. Somehow I felt that I had my foot in the door and that all would be well. The Quartermaster General sent for me and said so in so many words: 'The Secretary of State and you have put it across me. However I agree to the "Trooping" in full dress, but after that you must return to battledress for public duties. We cannot afford it.' Once in full dress I felt pretty certain that there was no return to wartime khaki for the public and press point of view.[2]

[2] Permission was given for full dress to be worn by the Household Cavalry for a Tattoo in Liverpool on 7–9 August 1947, and the King and the War Office agreed that a small mounted detachment should also be allowed to wear it for the Alexander Korda film *The Ideal Husband*.

King George VI, Colonel-in-Chief Coldstream Guards, taking the salute at the 1947 Birthday Parade. *Copyright reserved. Reproduced by gracious permission of Her Majesty The Queen*

75

But come the great day in 1948 when the Colour of the Major General's old battalion, the 2nd Battalion Scots Guards, was to be trooped, there was disaster.

Pouring rain and thunder from an early hour. The 'Met' report was bad for the rest of the day. At 9 a.m. a call from Buckingham Palace. What did I think? (It was, at that moment, quite black.) His Majesty is very dubious. I agree that the weather report holds out no hope at all and that the parade must be cancelled. From my house, I gave out the sad news to my Staff. Hardly had I done so, when a blazing sun appears and the rest of the day is perfect. Another call from Buckingham Palace. Can I cancel my cancellation of the parade? Too late—the Massed Bands have been dismissed and gone. Sadly I change into plain clothes and drive down to Horse Guards. As I enter the Mall, I am horrified. Great crowds are still there. I stop to ask a Senior Police Officer why the cancellation hasn't been given out by wireless van and loud speaker. He doesn't know and can hardly believe that it is a fact. Even more sadly do I enter my office and mentally pray for another thunderstorm. But in vain.

The Palace rings up to ask if we can put on the parade for the next day. Certainly, I reply. They will consult the weather experts and let me know. Later, I'm told that the outlook for the morrow is equally bad, and therefore it is of no use.

Trooping day was a Thursday—there was not a drop of rain until the Tuesday of the next week! So much for 'Met' reports, and don't we know them! Rather like Mary, Queen of Scots,[3] I have 'Trooping 1948' written on my heart forever. I don't think that the then Sergeant Major of the 2nd Battalion Scots Guards has ever forgiven me![4] That afternoon was the opening of the Royal Tournament[5] by His Majesty The King at Olympia. Quite frankly, I was terribly nervous at what His Majesty might say to me about the morning's decision. As he got out of the car and I saluted and shook him by the hand, he said, 'John, I think we made the right decision this morning.' I don't know how many readers knew the King

[3] Actually it was Mary Tudor who is alleged to have said, 'When I am dead, Calais will be found engraved on my heart.'

[4] The Subaltern and the Ensign of the Escort must have been equally sad. They were brothers: Lieutenant Lord Ogilvy, now the Earl of Airlie, Lord Chamberlain, and 2nd Lieutenant Hon. Angus Ogilvy, now Sir Angus, who married HRH The Princess Alexandra. The King wrote at once to their father commiserating. The Captain of No. 2 Guard *was* sad: he was the author of this history.

[5] As a result only four regimental bands were available for the Parade, the fifth being on duty at the Tournament.

76

well, but doesn't that remark convey to you a real person of under-standing, which he was? My morale was at once restored.

One who was thoroughly displeased was Mr Winston Churchill, now Leader of the Opposition, who complained that the Parade should only have been cancelled on the advice of a Minister. The Private Secretary replied, 'The King feels, as did his Father and Grandfather before him, that the Birthday Parade is essentially a function personal to the Sovereign, with which the Secretary of State for War has no direct concern. In the present instance the King himself took the responsibility for ordering the cancellation, having of course consulted the GOC London District and having acquainted himself with the latest meteorological news . . .'[6] Churchill replied at once.

As an old and devoted servant of the Crown, I do not feel that this was a fair responsibility to put upon the King. It is the business of Ministers to shield the Sovereign from all kinds of decisions which may arouse public controversy and feeling. The Secretary of State is equally responsible for advising or not advising on a matter affecting the movement of Troops, or the cost and difficulty of the replacement of uniforms if damaged . . . on this particular day more than a quarter of a million people had been waiting for hours in the streets and their disappointment was natural. The incident is now closed, but I remain of the opinion that steps should be taken to relieve the Sovereign of the invidious responsibility of decid-ing such a difficult matter, and that in future it should be borne by Ministers who can defend their actions, whether right or wrong, in Parliament.

In 1949, however, on Thursday 9 June, all was well, and the 1st Battalion Welsh Guards furnished the Escort, with the Commanding Officer as Field Officer. The whole Parade wore Home Service Clothing,[8] except for HRH The Princess Elizabeth who continued to be dressed as Colonel of her Regiment in the uniform which she had worn in 1947. The Household Cavalry, led by the Mounted Band, escorted the King from Buckingham Palace to the Horse Guards but did not take part in the Parade; the Mounted Band counter-marched at the Admiralty Arch and led the Escort back to Barracks during the Troop performed by the Massed Bands.

Because of ill health His Majesty drove in a carriage, and General Rodney Moore[9] has this recollection:

---

[6] RA. GVI PS39/TR, 15 June 1948.

[7] *Ibid*, 16 June 1948.

[8] Initially Musicians wore rank and file tunics, and it was not until 1965 that the 'wings' were restored. Their magnificent gold braided tunics and their distinctive short swords, sadly, were not. 'Home Service Clothing' in the technical description of 'Full Dress'.

[9] Grenadier Guards, the Major General 1957–1959.

King George VI driving to the Birthday Parade on 9 June, 1949. Owing to ill health, he attended the Parade driving in an open landau, and mounted a dais to take the Salute. *PRO HQ London District*

It was quite a battle with the King: he had the idea of doing the Parade in a Land-Rover. He did not like the open landau plan as he was apprehensive that the carriage horses might be restive when the March Past took place. He suggested that the horses should be taken out of the carriage at the Saluting base, but eventually it was agreed that he would use a carriage and dismount from it and mount a dais, which was rolled out from under the arch during the inspection. I have with me at Hampton Court Arnold who was the postillion controlling the pair of horses. He was connected to the Monarch by a line from his ear through the harness to the carriage where the King had a microphone through which he gave continuous instructions. Luckily Arnold had no way of replying.

As was his invariable custom, followed today by HM The Queen, the King paid detailed attention to every aspect of the Parade. 'The King noticed that paragraph 861 of Brigade Standing Orders was not followed on Thursday last and the Colonels of Regiments and Major General did not follow His Majesty into the Quadrangle, only Princess Elizabeth and the Duke of Gloucester doing so. The King wishes this paragraph to be complied with in future and all Colonels of Regiments and yourself (the Major General) to dismount in the Quadrangle.'[10]

The following correspondence between the King's Private Secretary and Major T. P. Butler, Brigade Major, is another example:

The King asked me this morning how long the men of the Escort on The King's Birthday have to go before they get their dinners. I have made enquiries from Colonel Billy Malcolm who tells me, as I had suspected, the men of the King's Guard get their dinners as soon as the Guard is changed which, on this particular day of the year, means that they get them pretty late. The really unfortunate ones are the sentries of the first relief who presumably do not get their dinners till two hours later. The King wondered whether this matter could be considered for future occasions and whether some method of feeding these men, or of providing a sufficient number of men who had already had their dinners to mount the first relief could be found.

The Major General agreed that the men for whom the King had expressed particular concern 'no doubt feel an aching void in their tummies' and suggested that the first relief should be mounted after one hour. 'The Major General said that in the old days when HM The King held a Review in the Long Valley at Aldershot the troops got no food for many a long hour.' Back came the reply that while the King took the point, 'their successors of the present day are not only younger men but they unfortunately enjoy a very much less sustaining diet in their everyday ration.'[11]

[10] RA. GVI PS39/TR, 14 June 1949. Sir Terence Nugent to Major General Marriott.
[11] *Ibid*, 10, 14 and 16 June 1949.

The 1949 Parade. Princess Elizabeth, Colonel Grenadier Guards, and the Duke of Gloucester, Colonel Scots Guards, arrive on Horse Guards. *PRO HQ London District*

Writing in the *Household Brigade Magazine* of this Parade, the Editor, Sir Charles Petrie, included the following comment:

It is much to be regretted on several grounds that the foreign Military Attachés no longer formed part of the royal cavalcade as in pre-war days, and on all sides are heard the hope expressed that this custom would not be allowed to fall into desuetude. Their brilliant uniforms were always a conspicuous feature of the Birthday Parade. On the other hand the retinue of Equerries and senior officers of the Brigade kept much better formation than was the case two years ago, when for the irreverent they called to mind a troop drawn from one of those regiments of irregular horse which the Crown used to take into its pay during the prosecution of Eastern campaigns in the eighteenth and early nineteenth centuries.

In the following year, 1950, the Grenadier Guards, whose turn it was to furnish the Escort, waived their place on the roster in favour of the Coldstream, because it was the Tercentenary of the formation of that Regiment. The Parade was watched by Queen Mary, whose grandfather, Frederick Adolphus, Duke of Cambridge, had been 14th Colonel of the Coldstream, and attended by Princess Elizabeth, while His Majesty, for the second year be-

The Escort to the Colour, furnished by the 2nd Battalion Scots Guards who in 1982 were in the Falklands Task Force, marches past the Queen in slow time during the 1987 Parade. The Ensign carrying the Queen's Colour which bears the Battle Honour 'Falklands 1982', is 2nd Lieutenant W. H. C. Swinton, whose father and grandfather also served in the Regiment. *PRO HQ London District*

The Sovereign's Birthday Parade at its most spectacular (*above and below*) as the Guards march past in slow and quick time. *PRO HQ London District*

After the Guards have reformed in their original positions, it is the turn of the Sovereign's Escort of the Household Cavalry to walk and trot past. The picture above was taken at the 1st Rehearsal in 1984, when the Band does not wear State Dress. (*Below*) The Farriers of The Blues and Royals and The Life Guards follow the Escort, carrying their axes. *PRO HQ London District*

The Massed Bands of the Household Cavalry salute the Queen after the Trot Past. *PRO HQ London District*

After the Parade, the King takes the Salute at the Palace, as the Colonels of the Grenadier and Scots Guards ride past. *PRO HQ London District*

cause of ill health, rode in an open semi-state landau. It was in this year that an important decision was made: Shortly after being appointed to command what was then called the Brigade of Guards, Major General Julian Gascoigne, Grenadier Guards, was told by the King that His Majesty wished him also to take under command the Household Cavalry, with the same responsibilities and privileges as the Foot Guards. Thus the Household Brigade was created, and to mark this the Major General proposed, and the King agreed, that the Household Cavalry should play a more important role in the Birthday Parade. As we have seen, in 1949 they had merely escorted the Sovereign to Horse Guards and then returned to barracks. Now the Sovereign's Escort, to the music of the Mounted Band, walked past and saluted the King after the final Royal Salute by the Foot Guards. They did the same at Buckingham Palace before the fly past by the Royal Air Force, which was also an innovation in London. (A section of the 'Royal Flying Corps Military Wing' did this for the first time at the King's Birthday Parade held on Laffan's Plain, Aldershot, in 1913.)

Lady Cynthia Colville, Lady-in-Waiting to Queen Mary, received a letter from a friend which Queen Mary said she should send to Sir Michael Adeane because 'in a spare moment—if such exist—the King might be interested'.

The Duke of Beaufort, Master of the Horse, and the Earl of Athlone, Gold Stick in Waiting, saluting Queen Mary as they pass Marlborough House after a rehearsal for the King's Birthday Parade on 8 June, 1950. *Copyright reserved. Reproduced by gracious permission of Her Majesty The Queen*

The letter read:

> My son, Major John Clay (Rifle Brigade) was at Trooping the Colour and behind him sat a man who said he came from Sydney, Australia. His neighbour asked him if he had been long in England. He replied, 'I arrived yesterday.' 'Are you making a long stay?' 'No, I am going back tomorrow. I only came over for this and it has cost me £680 but it has been worth it.' His Majesty has to hear so many unpleasant things these days, perhaps he would be cheered by such loyalty and devotion.[12]

The year 1951 was marked by the Festival of Britain, and the Birthday Parade coincided with the State Visit of King Haakon of Norway, who watched from the window of the Major General's office. King George VI had been advised by his doctors to rest, and HRH The Princess Elizabeth took the Salute, as Colonel of her Regiment, in full dress uniform, the style of which was to become so familiar. The King approved a request that the foreign Military Attachés should wear uniform in their stand. For the first time Prince Charles was there, driving with his royal grandmother in her carriage,

[12] *Ibid*, 1950. Sir Michael (later Lord) Adeane was the King's Private Secretary.

and for the first time the new Colour of the 3rd Battalion Grenadier Guards, which their Colonel had presented only a few days before, was trooped. On this Parade the Household Cavalry both walked and trotted past, after the Foot Guards and after the final Royal Salute, and the 1st Battalion Scots Guards, having relinquished their role as a training battalion for the Foot Guards at Pirbright, were on parade.[13]

Captain Nigel Nicolson, sometime a Grenadier Guardsman, recorded in the *Guards Magazine* his most marked impression of the occasion thus:

> But it was the bearing of the Princess Elizabeth more than her uniform which excited our deepest respect. It seemed to me that I was looking at a coloured print of a scene which might have happened at any period within the last 200 years. Here was an idealised portrait of the young Queen Victoria, calm, lovely, noble and intensely English, part of, and yet distinct from, the brilliant cavalcade which spun slowly behind her. Having ridden round the ranks, she took up her position facing the orderly mass of men, and the dress, masculine drill and shouted words of command became all the more impressive in contrast to the figure of the young girl at their head.

Later the Major General received the following message:

> Will you please inform all ranks that the King was delighted to hear my report on the Excellence of the King's Birthday Parade today. I was very proud to deputise for the King and take the Parade for the first time.
>
> Elizabeth
> Colonel, Grenadier Guards.[14]

On Tuesday 5 June 1952, as Colonel-in-Chief Scots Guards, for the first time in her own right, Her Majesty took the Salute when the Queen's Colour of the 2nd Battalion Scots Guards was trooped. In her hat she wore the Star of the Regiment, presented to her by members of the Third Guards Club, and it was by her express command that the pipers moved to the front of the Massed Bands to play as the Escort and No. 2 Guard marched past in quick time, and this custom continues. It was also the smallest parade to be held, with only five guards furnished because two Guards Brigades were stationed in Egypt and a third in Germany.[15] The Household Cavalry walked and trotted past

---

[13] In 1947 this Battalion trooped their Colour in Trieste. The following year they assumed their training role in England with companies from other regiments, and would have found one guard, furnished by 13 Company Grenadier Guards, if the Parade had not been cancelled. In 1949 the Battalion provided three guards: one by Right Flank, one by Headquarters Company and the third by 13 Company.

[14] RA. GVI PS39/TR, 7 June 1951.

[15] The number of Guards, eight, which are furnished today was not laid down until 1968; before that date the number varied: there were five guards in 1954, six in 1939 and seven in 1963 to 1967 inclusive.

The Queen's Birthday Parade on 11 June, 1953. HM The Queen, with HRH Prince Philip, Duke of Edinburgh in the uniform of a Field Marshal, takes the Salute outside the Palace. *S & G Press Agency*

before the final Royal Salute, and this has now become the accustomed practice.

The following year, 1953, was that of the Coronation on 2 June, and on the 11th the Colour of the 1st Grenadiers, which the Queen herself had presented the previous month, was trooped. Prince Philip was on parade in the full dress uniform of a Field Marshal for the first and last time; his 33rd birthday coincided with the 1954 Parade, by which date he had been appointed Colonel Welsh Guards.

Recalling the 1953 Parade, His Royal Highness writes:

> My horse did not behave particularly well. In fact I got so annoyed with it that I gave it a smart whack over the rump with my Field Marshal's baton—the only weapon at hand—as I went through the centre arch at Buckingham Palace. It did not make much impression on the horse but it bent the little figure of St George and I had a hefty bill for its repair!

In 1955 the Parade was cancelled because of a rail strike, and 1958 almost saw a repeat of the abortive 1948 Parade. On both these occasions it was the turn of the Scots Guards to troop their Colour—in 1958 the 1st Battalion. Despite heavy rain, however, the Birthday Parade was held. According to *The Times* of 13 June, 'Yesterday afternoon a Senior Staff Officer at London District Headquarters explained that the decision not to postpone the parade until the afternoon was made because the official weather forecast predicted light rain throughout the day until 4 p.m. and there would therefore be no certain advantage in delaying the parade.' The Adjutant in Brigade Waiting had hardly got back to Regimental Headquarters when he was rung up by the Press to be asked how much a tunic cost and how many had been ruined by the rain!

This was General Moore's first Parade as the Major General. 'The weather,' he related, 'was uncertain.'

> I don't think I worried about the meteorological reports but refused to make a decision to cancel before leaving Cadogan Gardens. I drove with Police Escort to Buckingham Palace where Michael Adeane met me and said the Queen wanted to see me. I went upstairs. I remember the Queen was in breeches and boots and a dark sweater, Prince Philip in overalls and shirt sleeves, and we looked out of the window. Prince Philip suggested we should cancel it. I said to the Queen, 'Madam, there is a very large crowd in the Mall.' Prince Philip suggested going cloaked for the ride up. I said it was only 13 minutes so I did not think it worthwhile. The Street Liners and Guards had their capes on. It was decided to go ahead, and I went down to the Quadrangle where all those taking part in the procession were waiting, mounted. I said to Prince Henry, 'We go, Sir.' He said, 'Who is going to pay for my tunic?' General Budget Loyd[16] said

---

[16] General Sir Charles Loyd, Colonel Coldstream Guards. Major General 1944–1947, uniquely in the rank of General.

something caustic. The Queen had the greatest reception in the Mall I have ever heard from a fairly damp crowd. The Troops had thrown off their capes and the girls behind them had put them on themselves, making a pretty back cloth.

We were five minutes late leaving and, of course, arriving on Horse Guards. It drizzled the whole time, and when the Guards got back into line after the quick March Past, I was just going to suggest to Her Majesty that we should call it a day when there was a slight let-up, so I let it go. We got back somewhat damp but well satisfied.

In 1959 the Parade was held on a Saturday—a day that since then has, for very practical reasons, been followed—and on that occasion the Colour of the 3rd Coldstream was trooped for the last time before the Battalion went into 'suspended animation', as was that of the 3rd Battalion Grenadier Guards the following year for the same reason. 'At the Queen's request,' writes Sir Rodney, 'we made every effort to cut down time and eliminated some of those unnecessary dressings so loved by Sergeant Majors, thus saving 13 minutes.'

In 1960 the new rifle was issued, and this posed some practical problems as the Duke of Edinburgh relates:

As I remember it, the Colonels went into Colour Court at St James's Palace to see the new rifle and to discuss any alterations to the arms drill that might be needed. A Drill Sergeant was there to demonstrate.

The cocking lever on the first versions of the self loading rifle or SLR (then known as the FN) had rather prominent knobs which stuck out on

The Regimental Adjutants of the Household Cavalry and the Foot Guards in the Quadrangle of Buckingham Palace before the first rehearsal for the 1959 Parade. *Francis-Thompson Ltd*

Following the 1959 Parade, the Queen returns to the Palace at the head of her Troops. *PRO HQ London District*

one side and made sloping arms uncomfortable as the knob went into the shoulder. I remembered seeing an eighteenth century print showing a party of Guardsmen marching across the Horse Guards with their rifles at the 'shoulder' and I also remembered that the Royal Marine Guards for the morning Colours marched onto the Quarterdeck with their rifles at the 'shoulder' to avoid poking their bayonets through the awning. So I suggested that the Drill Sergeant might try that position with the SLR. He seemed to find it quite comfortable, the Colonels thought that it was acceptable and so it was adopted.

I should add that there had been quite a long discussion about retaining the Lee-Enfield only for ceremonial purposes, but in the end it was agreed that it would make more sense for the Guards to use the contemporary equipment, particularly as all other regiments and services would have to convert to the new rifle.

As a result the new Major General, Sir George Burns, wrote to HRH the Senior Colonel as follows:

87

'Sergeant—tell that man if he removes his bearskin from his eyes he'll see that the rest of us finished Trooping the Colour last Thursday.' Cartoon by Giles. *Express Newspapers*

'Apart from the 209,000,000 Russians watching the Trooping on TV, I shall be watching—so this year we'll try it without half of you falling feet over head.' The Regimental Sergeant Major addresses the Escort from the 2nd Battalion Scots Guards, commanded by the author. Cartoon by Giles, 1961. *PRO HQ London District*

It has been my intention to make the minimum number of changes to the form of the Parade (as a result of the introduction of the new rifle), so as to see what it looks like for one year. After this we may have to think again, and I should be most grateful for any comments that you may have to make. However, there are three small changes that you will notice. Firstly, in order to allow the men a little more room in the ranks for marching past, I have reduced the size of each Guard by six men, as the width of a Guard cannot be any greater for the march past. Therefore you will notice that when in line the men will not be standing shoulder to shoulder.

Secondly, for marching off, each Guard will form into three divisions and not four as before. Owing to the reduction in size of the Queen's Guard, each detachment now consists of one division only. Therefore the St James's Palace Detachment of the Queen's Guard on June 11th will be the first division of the Escort, and the Buckingham Palace Detachment the third and last division of No. 8 Guard.[17]

1961, however, cannot be allowed to pass without a special mention. It was for the Grenadiers the first Birthday Parade to be attended by that distinguished Guardsman, the late Major General Sir Allan Adair, on his succession to the Colonelcy. It has been described as 'The Celtic Trooping'. *The Times* correspondent noted that 'of the eight guards, only one (from the 1st Coldstream) came from South of the Border or East of the Irish Channel'. The Queen's Colour of the 2nd Battalion Scots Guards was trooped, and Her Majesty and Their Royal Highnesses The Dukes of Edinburgh and Gloucester wore the Star and Sash of the Order of the Thistle. The parade was transmitted by television to Russia, provoking the following *Times* comment: 'As their Company Sergeant Major (Irish Guards) dressed the ranks (of the first Guard to arrive) and gave the "Eyes Front", it was thought that for the first time the voice of a Warrant Officer of the Brigade of Guards was being heard in the Kremlin. It hardly needed, one felt, the radio apparatus to carry it.' Queen Elizabeth The Queen Mother honoured the Field Officer in Brigade Waiting, and the officers of the Escort and New Guard, with her presence at luncheon in the Guard Room, St James's Palace, and Her Majesty wore as a brooch the badge of the Regiment of which her royal husband had been Colonel and, when King, Colonel-in-Chief.

The Duke of Edinburgh was not present the following year, 1962, which *The Times* described as 'vintage':

A distinguished officer of the Coldstream (the Colour of whose 2nd Battalion was trooped), wearing what was indisputedly his own morning

---

[17] Household Brigade letter DO/4927/Gen, of 1 June 1960. The Major General's third point in this letter mentioned that because of the Hyde Park Corner development scheme, the Household Cavalry would rank past the Queen in front of the Palace from left to right because they would have to return to barracks via Buckingham Palace Road.

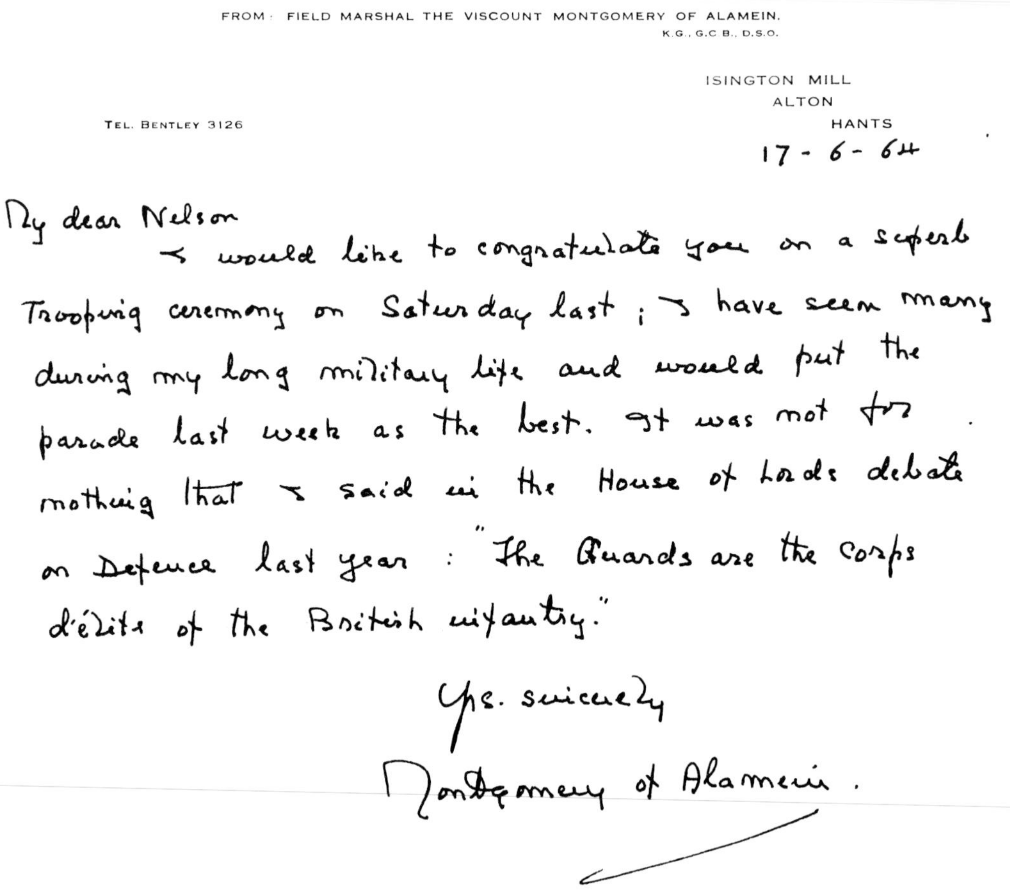

FROM: FIELD MARSHAL THE VISCOUNT MONTGOMERY OF ALAMEIN.
K.G., G.C.B., D.S.O.

ISINGTON MILL
ALTON
HANTS

TEL. BENTLEY 3126

17 - 6 - 64

My dear Nelson

I would like to congratulate you on a superb Trooping ceremony on Saturday last ; I have seen many during my long military life and would put the parade last week as the best. It was not for nothing that I said in the House of Lords debate on Defence last year : "The Guards are the corps d'élite of the British infantry."

Yrs. sincerely

Montgomery of Alamein.

Letter from Field Marshal the Viscount Montgomery of Alamein addressed to Major General John Nelson, Grenadier Guards, the Major General, after the 1964 Parade.

coat, said that it was the best Queen's Birthday Parade for years; a Grenadier Captain admitted that it was not bad. For the connoisseur this was a vintage year for the Trooping . . . It was perhaps only a touch of Celtic twilight in one observer that made the Scots fractionally the best of eight magnificent Guards . . . The Minister of Defence looked relaxed, safe in the knowledge that in the unlikely event of anything going wrong, for once no one could possibly blame him.

In 1963, with the end of National Service and an increase in the commitments for the Foot Guards overseas, the Mall was lined by recruits from the Guards Depot for the first and last time, and in 1964 the Ground Keepers (seven officers and 110) were dispensed with.

The Queen arrives for the 1964 Birthday Parade, when the Colour was trooped by the 1st Battalion Coldstream Guards. *PRO HQ London District*

The Parade of 1964 was the last that the Duke of Gloucester attended. He had succeeded his brother, the King, as Colonel Scots Guards in 1937 and had been Senior Colonel for many years. His knowledge of the Foot Guards was profound and a newly appointed Equerry, on his first visit to Barnwell Manor, recalls playing a game of canasta after dinner, throughout which Prince Henry wore his bearskin cap in order to ensure a good fit for the Parade—a habit which the late King also followed: he wore his while gardening at Royal Lodge, and the Duke of Windsor, when Prince of Wales and King Edward VIII, did the same.[18]

Before the Trooping in 1965, Major General John Nelson, who was at that time the Major General, relates that:

> The weather forecast was abysmal and there was rain and thunder all the night before. Having witnessed John Marriott's dilemma in 1948 and also aware of the fact that even after the Coronation procession in 1953 when tunics were worn for four hours in pouring rain throughout, only 3

[18] The Duke of Windsor recalls: 'When my brother, the Duke of York, was appointed Colonel of the Scots Guards and thus had to wear a bearskin for the first time, I strongly advised him to follow my example. Unfortunately he chose to disregard my advice, remarking, "I have tried it on and it seems to fit perfectly well!" Retribution fell upon him not long afterwards at the King's Birthday Parade. The cap began to give him such pain that he was obliged to withdraw from the Parade, dismounting and relieving his head for a while before he could continue and resume his place. Already piqued at his discomfiture, he was still less pleased when I afterwards chaffed him with the irresistible comment, "I told you so!" ' *A Family Album*. HRH The Duke of Windsor. Cassell, 1960.

In 1965 it was the turn of the 1st Battalion Welsh Guards. The Queen as Colonel-in-Chief and the Duke of Edinburgh, Colonel Welsh Guards, ride on to Horse Guards. *PRO HQ London District*

per cent of them were irretrievably spoilt, I was determined never to cancel a Parade for which I was responsible because of bad weather. It was still raining at 10 a.m. but I managed to get a forecast from the RAF for Central London which predicted rain all day except between 11 a.m. and 1 p.m. When I met the Colonels mounting their horses in pouring rain outside the Guardroom at Buckingham Palace, a very senior Field Marshal, Sir Gerald Templer,[19] scowled at me and declared that I must be out of my mind not to call it off. At 10.50, as the Queen came out of the Palace to mount her charger, the rain stopped and did not start again until she had dismounted two hours later. Weather forecasting had improved since 1948.

He also recorded that in that year flagpoles were first erected for the flags of the Commonwealth: 'When I first noticed them from my office window, I sent

[19] Colonel at that time of The Royal Horse Guards (The Blues), who amalgamated four years later with The Royals, to become The Blues and Royals.

In perfect formation the Massed Bands of Her Majesty's Foot Guards march across the ground.
PRO HQ London District

for Philip Ward, my Brigade Major, and said, "Those flags are far too low. The Queen's horse might well shy at them. Whose stupid idea was it to have them anyway?" To which he replied, "Yours, Sir"!'

The form of the Parade now became established, and the subsequent changes merely added to perfection by simplicity. For example, the Queen herself decided shortly before the 1963 Ceremony, much to the relief of some, that the Regimental Lieutenant Colonels of Foot Guards, their Adjutants and Silver Stick Adjutant should no longer form part of the 'Inspection Procession', but take up their positions in front of the Horse Guards Building; in 1971, the fifes of the Corps of Drums were so pitched that they could play with the massed bands; in 1972 the number of divisions found by each Guard was reduced from three to two, and as a result the Escort to the Colour furnished both detachments of the New Guard; and, to avoid unnecessary delay, the Field Officer no longer waited for the drummer to return to his position in the

93

The Queen returns down the Mall after the 1967 Birthday Parade and, with the Duke of Edinburgh beside her, takes the Salute. *PRO HQ London District*

Band after beating the Drummer's Call[20] before ordering the Escort for the Colour to shoulder arms and take close order. For the same reasons, too, in 1973 it was decided that the Escort should not be dressed after they had returned to their position on the right of the Line after Trooping the Colour: they halted, turned to the front and at once presented arms. And more recently, in 1978, in order to relieve the tedium of the 'Grenadiers' March' which hitherto had been played for six minutes, with the Queen's approval an arrangement of Waldteufel's 'Grenadier Waltz' was added. This is now played from the time the Escort advances *with* the Colour until the music stops to allow the Field Officer to order the Guards to present arms.

[20] An early reference to this Call is given in *Military Discipline* by Humphrey Bland, 1759: 'The officers having taken their position in the front of the Battalion, and the ranks and files being dressed, the Colours are then sent for; which is usually performed in the following manner: the Major is to order one of the Grenadier Drummers to beat the Drummer's Call; upon which the Ensigns who are to carry the Colours are to report to the head of the Company of Grenadiers.' Today, on this Call, the Subaltern takes over command from the Captain of the Escort (furnished by the Flank or Grenadier Company) before advancing with the Ensign and the Escort to receive the Colour.

The Queen rides to the Saluting base to be received by a Royal Salute. *PRO HQ London District*

Trooping the Colour, 1968, by the 2nd Battalion Coldstream Guards. *PRO HQ London District*

The Major General commanding the Household Division, Lord Michael Fitzalan-Howard, at the 2nd Rehearsal in 1969—the last opportunity to spot the faults and put them right before the day. *PRO HQ London District*

Five events, however, deserve especial mention: On the 1969 Parade the Queen first rode Burmese, who was born in 1962 at the Royal Canadian Mounted Police Stud at Regina in Western Canada, and, at the age of six was selected to lead the RCMP musical ride. In 1969 the RCMP came over to perform at the Royal Windsor Horse Show and it was then that she was presented to the Queen. Shortly afterwards the Duke of Edinburgh rode her at the rehearsal for the Trooping and she was considered a safe and suitable mount for Her Majesty. In the space of three weeks Burmese was trained by Mrs Doreen Archer-Houblan to carry a side saddle, and in subsequent years she was given refresher training from Miss Sylvia Stanier. The Queen rode her on eighteen Birthday Parades until 1986.[21]

---

[21] Because riding side saddle necessitates using muscles not normally exercised, Her Majesty would start practising regularly at the end of April or early May, especially at Windsor, and then in the Riding School and Garden of Buckingham Palace three or four times a week for an hour at a time.

After the Parade, HM Queen Elizabeth The Queen Mother and other members of the Royal Family return to the Palace. (*Above*) The Queen Mother with HRH Princess Anne returning from the 1976 Parade. *PRO HQ London District*

Placing herself at the head of her Guards, HM The Queen returns down the Mall to the Palace after the 1976 Parade. *PRO HQ London District*

A panorama of colour and pageantry as the Procession nears the Palace, filling the Mall with ordered ranks of Foot Guards and Household Cavalry. Riding beside the Queen after the 1981 Parade is HRH the Duke of Edinburgh, Colonel Grenadier Guards, and behind her the Colonels of the Coldstream, Welsh and Scots Guards, and the Major General. *PRO HQ London District*

At the Palace gates the Queen turns to take the Salute as her Guards march past. Until 1987 the Salute was taken mounted, but in 1987 the Queen alighted from her phaeton and stood on a dais to take the Salute. Mounted is Lieutenant Colonel Julian Lancaster, Field Officer in Brigade Waiting, who commanded the Parade, and standing is Lieutenant Colonel Blair Stewart Wilson, the Equerry in Waiting, both of the Scots Guards. *PRO HQ London District*

The Queen about to take the Salute of the King's Troop, Royal Horse Artillery. *PRO HQ London District*

HM The Queen, Colonel-in-Chief, with the Colonels of Regiments of the Household Division, after the 1986 Parade. Left to right: Major General Lord Michael Fitzalan-Howard (The Life Guards); Major General Sir George Burns (Coldstream Guards); the Prince of Wales (Welsh Guards); the Duke of Edinburgh (Grenadier Guards); the Duke of Kent (Scots Guards); the Grand Duke of Luxembourg (Irish Guards); General Sir Desmond Fitzpatrick (The Blues and Royals). *PRO HQ London District*

The Royal Family on the Balcony after the 1987 Parade. *PRO HQ London District*

Miss Sylvia Stanier riding Burmese at the 2nd Rehearsal, 1970. *PRO HQ London District*

Secondly, in 1970 by roster the 2nd Battalion Grenadier Guards should have trooped their Colour, but because, on the reorganisation of the Army, the Foot Guards were forced to sacrifice a battalion, they surrendered the privilege to the 2nd Battalion Scots Guards whose demise was then imminent (but later restored)—a gesture which demonstrated the singular 'family feeling' which permeates the Division. Thirdly, shortly before the Parade of 1972 HRH The Duke of Windsor died, and a Special Notice was inserted in the official programme edged in mourning black, which read thus:

> On the Queen's Command, Her Majesty's Birthday Parade this year will incorporate an Act of Remembrance for the late Duke of Windsor. There-fore, immediately after the arrival of Her Majesty The Queen on parade, there will be a roll of drums. This will be followed by a minute's silence, which will be followed by a second roll of drums. After this, the Pipes will play a Lament. After the Lament, Her Majesty will receive a Royal Salute and the Parade will continue as usual.[22]

The fourth event was the decision that after the King's Troop had fired the Salute in Hyde Park they would form up and rank past the Queen at Bucking-ham Palace, preceding the Household Cavalry. And the fifth was the appoint-ment in 1974 of HRH The Duke of Edinburgh[23] to the Colonelcy of the Grenadier Guards, and his succession in the Welsh Guards by Prince Charles.

Lieutenant Colonel (now Major General) Charles Guthrie, Welsh Guards, was Brigade Major in 1976 and 1977 and recalls that a list of events including the dates of Beating Retreat, Guard Mounting from Horse Guards, Re-hearsals and the Birthday Parade, early morning practices and so on, was sent over to No. 10 Downing Street. 'It was not the practice for the list to be queried but we always did it as a matter of courtesy.'

In 1976 an incensed Superintending Clerk had been telephoned by Number 10 and told to 'switch the music off'. A Cabinet Meeting was in progress and those present could not concentrate. And he relates that the following year the Prime Minister's wife had requested that there should be no early morn-ing rehearsals as the band woke up her husband who needed his rest. 'As you know, in the "silly season" there is not much room for manoeuvre, so the Staff Captain and I went across to Downing Street one afternoon and discussed the problem. We managed without too much difficulty to alter the times to when

---

[22] There has only been one other 'Silence': on 11 June 1982 for the Falklands Task Force (see p. 109).

[23] Prince Philip's Grenadier Guards sword is that which King Edward VII carried when, as Prince of Wales, he served with the Regiment in Ireland at the Curragh in 1861. Four Field Marshals' swords are carried by officers of the Irish Guards: that of Lord Roberts (first Colonel of the Regiment) by the Lieutenant Colonel, the Earl of Ypres by the Commanding Officer, the Earl of Cavan by the Battalion Adjutant, and Earl Alexander of Tunis by the Regimental Adjutant. The names of those who first carried them are on the flat of the blade, and of those whose appointments entitle them to do so on the reverse.

the Prime Minister was away, and all parties were satisfied. I do remember that Mrs (now Lady) Callaghan was thoroughly reasonable about her request and apologetic, but believed that Jim should not overdo it! She behaved like a proper wife.'[24]

The Queen's Silver Jubilee was celebrated in 1977 when a Conference of Commonwealth Prime Ministers was held in London. Two stands were occupied behind 10 Downing Street so that the visitors, as guests of the Prime Minister, could watch the Birthday Parade: the Heads of Government were seated in one and the High Commissioners in the other.

Major General Sir James Eyre[25] recalls an event at the end of the 1978 Parade when he was riding back down the Mall.

[24] This situation was not new: In October 1733 Scrope, the Treasury Minister, whose department occupied a new building to the south of Horse Guards, wrote to the Secretary at War: 'The exercising of soldiers which is almost every day now done before the Treasury at Whitehall in the morning when the Treasury Lords are sitting, and with drums beating, gives great disturbance to the business of the office. It is therefore their Lordships' desire that the said exercise with drums be performed in some other place.' It was not.

[25] The Blues and Royals. The second Household Cavalry officer to have been appointed the Major General (1983–1986).

The 1971 Parade: in the Queen's procession (*left*) the Duke of Beaufort, Master of the Horse and the Earl Mountbatten of Burma, Colonel The Life Guards. After the Inspection of the Line, the Brigade Major and four Troopers (*right*) lead the Queen's procession back to the Saluting base. *PRO HQ London District*

The 1972 Birthday Parade took place shortly after the death of HRH The Duke of Windsor. Here the Guards march past the Queen who, like all the officers, is wearing a mourning band. *PRO HQ London District*

Behind No. 8 Guard rode the Major of the Parade, the Adjutant in Brigade Waiting; behind them were the Master of the Horse (the Duke of Beaufort—'Master'), Gold Stick (Earl Mountbatten of Burma—'Colonel Dicky'), the Colonel of The Blues and Royals (Field Marshal Sir Gerald Templer) and myself as Silver Stick, with the Lieutenant Colonels and Regimental Adjutants of Foot Guards bringing up the rear. I suddenly noticed that Colonel Dicky was advancing more rapidly than the rest of us. Of course Master and the Field Marshal did nothing out of mischief. The necks of the Major and Adjutant in Brigade Waiting reddened perceptibly as they were joined by Gold Stick and even more so as he passed between them, joining up with the rear rank of No. 8 Guard. The comments from behind me were not exactly helpful! Eventually I pushed on and asked Colonel Dicky if he was feeling all right (I thought he could be having a heart attack). 'I am perfectly all right,' he replied. I therefore suggested that he rejoin the Household Cavalry and permit No. 8 Guard to proceed on its way in peace. He said nothing but reined back. Afterwards he came up to me in the Quadrangle of Buckingham Palace and thanked me, saying, 'I was lost in my thoughts as I was composing a speech.' I said nothing but was rather sceptical. However, that night The

At the conclusion of the Parade the Queen takes the final Salute as the Foot Guards march past, the Household Cavalry walk past and the King's Troop Royal Horse Artillery rank past. *PRO HQ London District*

With so many people involved, much quiet consultation goes on between individuals. a. The experts have a point! b. The Major General assures the Colonels Coldstream Guards and The Blues and Royals that all is well. c. The Colonel The Blues and Royals, Gold Stick, checks up with Silver Stick. d. The Chief of Staff checks with the Groom that his charger will, hopefully, behave. *PRO HQ London District*

Life Guards held their Association Dinner at Windsor. That year he gave an original and witty speech—the first time he had departed from his 'Winston and I' theme. So perhaps he was right!'[26]

The following year it was decided that Lord Mountbatten as Colonel of The Life Guards would take the Salute at the 2nd Rehearsal. The Prince of Wales, however, had expressed his intention of riding on this parade. 'This,' wrote Major General John Swinton, Commanding the Household Division, to HRH the Duke of Edinburgh, Senior Colonel, 'produces an interesting and, as far as I can discover, unprecedented situation of a Royal Colonel attending a Non Royal Colonel on such a rehearsal.' He sought confirmation that he was interpreting Her Majesty's Regulations for the Household Division as the Queen, through the Senior Colonel, would wish:

> That because of the presence of the Prince of Wales the order of dress should be as laid down for the presence of a member of the Royal Family; and that the Buckingham Palace Detachment of the Queen's Guard should turn out in the Forecourt of the Palace on the return of the procession and give a Royal Salute to His Royal Highness as he rode into the Quadrangle.

On the other hand he proposed that as the Salute would be taken by the Colonel of The Life Guards the Regimental Colour should be trooped, that neither the Standard nor Colour be lowered, and that Lord Mountbatten should be accorded a General Salute.

This was agreed and set a precedent for 1980 when the Prince of Wales again was present at the 2nd Rehearsal and the Salute was taken by General Sir Basil Eugster, Colonel Irish Guards.

Lieutenant Colonel Sir John Miller, Welsh Guards, was appointed Crown Equerry in 1961 and attended sixty-four rehearsals for the Birthday Parade and the Parade itself. By nature he would not seem to be a superstitious man, but the number 13 fills him with some apprehension. The 1981 Birthday Parade was held on 13th June, a day which he particularly, but many others too, will not easily forget. He recalls that on that occasion, before the Parade took place it was reported to him that the Duke of Edinburgh's charger had gone lame and that his groom had been injured in an accident. At the end of the Parade Queen Elizabeth The Queen Mother slipped on the stairs as she was leaving the Major General's Office in Horse Guards building, but the event which secured 'World News Status', which presumably was the purpose

---

[26] He was succeeded on his death by Major General Lord Michael Fitzalan Howard Scots Guards, who has been present at the Birthday Parades, uniquely, as Brigade Major, Chief of Staff London District, the Major General and Colonel The Life Guards and Gold Stick. He was, moreover, the last Brigade Major, Brigade of Guards, and first of the Household Brigade, and last Major General Commanding the Household Brigade and first the Household Division. (See Appendix 4.)

of the perpetrator, was when a young man in the crowd, at the junction of the Mall and the Approach Road, fired 'blanks' from a starting pistol at the Queen. Lance Corporal Galloway, Left Flank 2nd Battalion Scots Guards, from Edinburgh, a Scots Guardsman of thirteen years' service—which included a tour with the Guards Parachute Company and five on operations in Northern Ireland—was a Street Liner at that point. In the words of his Company Commander, Major John Kiszeley, himself to be a Falklands hero, 'he reacted fast and had no thought for his own safety'. 'I was at the present,' recalled Corporal Galloway. 'The Queen was about seven yards away. There was a noise which I thought was the crowd clapping; then I recognised it was gunfire—it sounded like 9 millimetre. I turned round and saw a man pointing a gun at the Queen, and as I turned he fired the last shot. The crowd was shouting and he was being pushed forward. I leaned across the barrier, grabbed him by the hair and pulled him into the Mall (where he was seized by the Police). I returned to my position.'

Not surprisingly, this incident, which was unprecedented in the history of the Birthday Parade and which might well have had fatal consequences, drew wide attention and admiration for the composure of the Queen. It also resulted in considerable correspondence in the Press. 'Where were The Life Guards?' asked one writer to *The Times* of 17 June. 'Until then I had held the romantic idea that if the Sovereign were threatened, the Cavalry Escort would immediately spur their horses forward to form a protective ring, guarding her with their own bodies.'[27]

On the same day, a retired Gloucestershire Colonel chided the Editor: 'You have overlooked the most effective and appropriate protection for members of the Royal Family: a close escort of big men on tall horses. The 2nd Life Guards should be reraised immediately'—and upon the file copy in the Archives of Headquarters Household Division were written the words 'Hear! Hear!'[28]

A reader of the *Daily Telegraph* proposed that Corporal Galloway should be honoured with the 'ancient' title of 'Queen's Corporal', which was warmly supported by a letter to *The Times* from Lt. Col. Naylor of Northamptonshire: 'I, and very many old soldiers, have long regretted the loss of the rank and honour of "Queen's Corporal". The rank carried with it certain privileges and the person retained the rank until his death.' Two days later, however, on 24 June, the Colonel's (and Corporal Galloway's) hopes were dashed by a letter to *The Times* from Sir Arthur Drew, who had been the last Permanent Under Secretary of State of the War Office and who recalled that the then Secretary of State for War, on 10 October 1944, had been asked in the House of Commons for every possible detail of 'King's Corporals', to which he replied, 'Extensive investigations have failed to disclose any factual basis for the

---

[27] The *Guards Magazine* (Summer 1981): 'The Field Officer of the Escort and the Standard Party rode forward to cover the Queen . . .'
[28] In 1922 the 1st and 2nd Life Guards had been amalgamated and called 'The Life Guards (1st and 2nd)' until 1928 when they were renamed 'The Life Guards'.

The 1979 Birthday Parade. Queen Elizabeth The Queen Mother and Princess Margaret drive on to the Parade Ground. *PRO HQ London District*

Colonel Simon Cooper, Silver Stick, gives the Foot Guards some last-minute advice before the 2nd Rehearsal for the Birthday Parade on 7 June, 1980. *PRO HQ London District*

The 1980 Parade. The Brigade Major salutes the Colour, riding at the head of the Queen's procession. *PRO HQ London District*

The 1980 Birthday Parade. Major General Desmond Langley, the first Household Cavalry officer to be appointed Major General commanding the Household Division, at the Palace before the 2nd Rehearsal with General Sir Desmond Fitzpatrick, Colonel The Blues and Royals and Gold Stick. *PRO HQ London District*

Left: The 1980 Birthday Parade. Prince Philip, wearing the sword of the Prince of Wales, later Edward VII, with two of the Queen's Equerries in the Quadrangle of the Palace. *Right*: The Guards step off in Divisions to march down the Mall after the 1981 Parade. *PRO HQ London District*

suggestion made from time to time that there is, or has been within living memory, any such rank as King's Corporal.' And Sir Arthur concluded that 'Colonel Naylor's letter suggests that the ghost walks again'! Corporal Galloway in fact received the Commendation of the GOC London District for his conduct.

As a result of this incident, security precautions were imposed for the future. These included the introduction of special radio communications, the order that police officers both on the route and on the ground should face the spectators, and finally a rigorous check of those attending the Parade to ensure that they and their bags or camera cases are innocuous.

It was planned that for the Parade in 1982 there should be eight Guards furnished as follows: the Escort and Number 2 Guard, 1st Battalion Coldstream Guards; Numbers 3 and 4, 1st Battalion Grenadier Guards; Numbers 5 and 6, 1st Battalion Welsh Guards; and Numbers 7 and 8, 2nd Battalion Scots Guards.

This had to be altered radically when, just over two weeks before the 1st Rehearsal, the Scots and Welsh Guards sailed for the South Atlantic as part of the Task Force which also included two troops of The Blues and Royals. The number of Guards was reduced to six and the 2nd Battalion Grenadier Guards had to furnish Numbers 5 and 6 Guards within a short time of returning from

107

Members of the Royal Party on the balcony of the Palace after the 1981 Parade. Queen Elizabeth The Queen Mother turns to Lady Diana Spencer, soon to become Princess of Wales. *PRO HQ London District*

their operational role in Germany as mechanised infantry. Two days after the 1st Rehearsal the Falklands Foot Guards battalions landed.

Major General Desmond Langley, who was the Major General commanding the Household Division at that time, has this recollection:

> After the 2nd Rehearsal (Saturday 5 June) I became aware that The Queen's Birthday Parade might well coincide with a battle. The Parachute Regiment's action at Goose Green had already resulted in casualties, and I was concerned that we might be judged insensitive if the Parade proceeded in the normal way without any recognition being given to operations 8,000 miles away in which those who would have been present on Horse Guards were taking part.
>
> On 9 June I consulted some of the Colonels of the Regiments of the Household Division, suggesting that there should be a 'Silence' at the beginning of the Parade, after which the Drums should sound the Last Post and Reveille. They agreed in principle and I went to discuss the proposal with the Queen's Private Secretary. That evening I heard the first reports of the tragic loss of life in 1st Battalion Welsh Guards incurred the previous day aboard the *Sir Galahad* at Fitzroy (39 missing presumed dead and 87 wounded).

I was told that after consultation the Queen had decided that there should be a Silence but that the bugle calls should not be sounded, and this seemed to me to be more appropriate as I knew that the main, and critical attack was to be launched at about the same time as the Ceremony was taking place in London. Accordingly I ordered this signal to be despatched:

> Subject is Queen's Birthday Parade. After her Majesty has been received on parade with a Royal Salute and the Guards have ordered arms, there will be a one minute's Silence when our thoughts are with all members of Her Majesty's Armed Forces, the Merchant Navy and others in the South Atlantic.

I had plenty to think about as I sat on my horse; the Silence seemed a bit too silent for me, and I was glad that I had directed the bands to play 'Hielan' Laddie' (Quick March of the Scots Guards) and 'The Rising of the Lark' (Welsh Guards) as the Queen rode off at the head of her Guards.

A monsoon took place as we passed St James's on our way down the Mall and saluted the Queen at Buckingham Palace. Major General Lord Michael Fitzalan-Howard's Household Cavalry jackboots were full of water when he took them off. The Duke of Edinburgh rode Solomon, one of his competition carriage horses, and that evening drove him in his team for the Coaching Club Dinner at Hampton Court—and got soaked again. ('I rather doubt,' he recalls, 'whether this has ever been done before, and it is unlikely to be done again.') When it was over the Queen sent me the following message:

> My thanks and congratulations to all those who took part in today's Parade. I felt a special pride this year when our thoughts were directed to those who are away in the South Atlantic, especially the Welsh and the Scots Guards who were so much missed from Horse Guards this morning.
>
> Please convey to the Escort for the Colour and to All Ranks on parade, including the Sovereign's Escort, the King's Troop, the Massed Bands and the Street Liners, my deep appreciation of their birthday tribute. Despite the downpour at the beginning and end, the Parade itself was impeccable. I hope that the ravages of the weather have not caused too much damage to uniforms and kit.

1983 was the last Parade attended by General Sir Basil Eugster as Colonel Irish Guards. He died in April 1984 and His Royal Highness The Grand Duke of Luxembourg was not appointed in his place till August of that year. The new Colonel, the Regiment's seventh, had been commissioned into the Irish Guards in 1943 and had served with their 3rd Battalion in the Guards Armoured Division until the relief of Brussels. He was the first Royal Colonel to be appointed who was not a member of the British Royal Family.

Many spectators may think that the part played by the Foot Guards' Bands has remained unchanged over the years, but with the formation of the Regimental Bands and Corps of Drums of the Irish and Welsh Guards (and the Pipes and Drums of the former) it became impossible for this mass of men, numbering well over 400, to manoeuvre in the customary manner, and as a result the 'Spin-Wheel' was invented. It is the responsibility of the Garrison Sergeant Major to ensure by rehearsals that it is executed correctly, and Lieutenant Colonel Rodney Bashford, late Director of Music Grenadier Guards, describes it:

A 'wheel' is not an easy manoeuvre with even a small body of troops, and with a block of 400 men the normal wheel is impossible. The massed band therefore pivots on its own centre, so that certain outer ranks and files march long distances in a hurry while the centre and inner ranks loiter with extreme intent, or merely mark time. Yet others not only step sideways but backwards as well. This highly complex movement is called a 'spin-wheel', the *details* of which can be found in no drill book or manual of ceremonial. Its complexity defies description, and if the truth were known, many of the participants know not whither they go or, on arrival, how they got there. The spin-wheel is almost an art form and each performance of it, although similar in essentials, is different in detail. Most of the performers are adjusting their actions to suit the needs of the spin-wheel of the moment, having adjusted their movements quite otherwise on other occasions.

The public is, hopefully, unaware of all this, and unless forewarned will as likely as not miss the action completely, for it all looks so simple and inevitable from a spectator's seat. The public is, also hopefully, unaware of events in the epicentre of that elegantly spinning body of men. The spectator hears only the music, but those on parade in the vicinity of the spin-wheel are aware of a deafening cacophony of crotchets and quavers plus much shouting and gesticulating as the five directors of music, hidden within the ranks, and the senior NCOs bid to control the wanderings of the less experienced brethren, lost to the world in what to them must resemble a super-orchestrated fairground roundabout gone mad. And as this spinning, roaring mass slowly gains equilibrium the raw ones are suddenly, frighteningly conscious of something amiss—a slight miscalculation perhaps on someone's part—for half the band is facing north, and the other south. Then a distant, ghostly scream, seemingly emanating from a euphonium to the north, effects an about turn by the eastern half. And all is finished.

The massed bands, corps of drums, and pipes and drums of Her Majesty's Guards Division have changed direction.

Opposite: The sun doesn't always shine on the Queen's Birthday Parade! Her Majesty with the Field Officer in Brigade Waiting riding back to the Palace after the 1982 Parade. *Ron Bell, PA Photos*

The Spin-Wheel. *Times Newspapers Ltd*

The 1984 Birthday Parade: the
Escort slow march along the ranks of
the Guards who present arms. *PRO
HQ London District*

During the Ceremony of Beating Retreat on Horse Guards Parade by the Bands, Corps of Drums and Pipes and Drums of the Household Division in 1986, the Queen, who was taking the Salute, remarked to the Major General who was sitting on the dais with her, about the direction of countermarching. Her Majesty pointed out that the Foot Guards bands go left about while the Royal Marines go right about, and then the Queen noticed that the pipers, to confuse matters, went left about when massed with the Regimental Bands and right about when on their own. The Major General had to admit that he did not know (and the author of this book, who also took the Salute of the same Ceremony in the same year, had not even noticed despite nearly 44 years as a Guardsman). Research was set in train and the following answers were sent to the Palace which the Major General described as 'logical':

Lieutenant Colonel John Mackenzie Rogan, Coldstream Guards, was the first Commissioned Director of Music. In 1920 he ordered that when Bass and Tuba players made up the front rank of Foot Guards bands, because their instruments were held across the body from left hip to right shoulder their view was blocked to the right and the bands would therefore countermarch to the left.

In the Corps of Drums the playing position of the flautists is such that their heads are inclined to the left and the dressing is always taken from the left. The *Drummers' Handbook* published in 1985 states that Corps of Drums are to countermarch to the left. When pipers are playing, the drones generally are over the left shoulder and it is, therefore, easier for them to countermarch to the right, obviating the possibility of drones

One of the most spectacular moments of the ceremony: the Pause when the Escort has marched out and received the Colour. *PRO HQ London District*

clashing in the act of countermarching. When the Pipes are massed with the Bands, however, they conform to the latter and countermarch to the left, but it is comparatively rare for them to be playing.

If there is one man, apart from the Field Officer in Brigade Waiting, upon whom a heavier responsibility lies than any other on parade, that man is the Senior Drum Major of the Foot Guards. It is he who, quite apart from directing the Spin-Wheel, determines when the Massed Bands should move and whither they should go, and it is he who by failing to stop the music at the appropriate moment could render the Field Officer totally inaudible.[29]

Up to 1970, whenever a Household Cavalry Mounted Band had taken part in the Parade, it had been furnished by one of the Regiments at a strength of a Director of Music, Drum Horse and thirty-six musicians. In 1971, however, the Bands of both Regiments were massed, under the command of the Senior Director of Music, with two drum horses carrying respectively the kettle-drums of The 1st Life Guards and The Blues and Royals and forty-eight musicians. 'This,' recorded *The Blue and Royal Magazine* of that year, 'made a great improvement to our tonal qualities and volume of sound, despite causing slight equestrian movement problems.'

In early years the Regiments of the Household Cavalry had only trumpeters and kettle-drummers who were mounted on grey horses, and with the introduction of other instrumentalists this custom was continued. After the First World War, because of a shortage of 'greys' all the horses were black except for a few files, and today the rear rank is composed of clarinet players on 'greys'.[30]

It is interesting to conjecture what might have happened if Lord Kitchener had survived the First World War and been able to carry out his intentions of keeping the Guards Division in existence in peacetime. As Lord Cavan, who had commanded the Division, wrote in his unpublished memoirs, 'When I saw three Arms—Cavalry, Artillery and Infantry—mounting the King's Guard in Madrid, I had my regrets . . . that the plan was stopped', and in a Minute to the King dated 7 April 1920, Winston Churchill, Secretary of State for War,

---

[29] All Foot Guards Drum Majors and Pipe Majors hold warrants as Household Drummers and Pipers to the Queen and it is for that reason that the former wear State Clothing. What is not so well known is that up to 1830 there was a 'Drum Major General' whose origins seem to have been in the Royal Household post of 'Major Drumplayer in ordinary'. The last two holders of this appointment were Drum Major Charles Stuart (3rd Foot Guards) and Drum Major William Hood (Coldstream).

[30] The Kettle Drums of the Blues and Royals are inscribed 'Given by King George III April 23 1805 to the Royal Regiment of Horse Guards on a testimonial of its honourable and military conduct on all occasions'. Those of The 2nd Life Guards, which are kept at Windsor and not carried on the Birthday Parade, are inscribed 'Presented by His Majesty William IV to the 2nd Regiment of Life Guards 1830' and were presented in the Home Park on 6 May 1831. Those of The 1st Life Guards are similarly and appropriately inscribed and were presented in the Little Park on 23 July 1831.

Since 1971 the drum horses of both The Life Guards and The Blues and Royals have taken part in the Parade. Here the Kettle-Drummers salute the Major General on his Rehearsal in 1984. *PRO HQ London District*

115

The Massed Mounted Bands of the Household Cavalry. *PRO HQ London District*

Over the years the central themes of the Birthday Parade have remained unchanged. *PRO HQ London District*

The Queen leaves the Parade Ground accompanied by members of the Royal Family who hold appointments in the Foot Guards, Colonels of Regiments of Foot Guards, the Major General and her Equerries. *PRO HQ London District*

explained why, for very practical reasons, the proposal could not be supported. And paradoxically it was Churchill who, while advocating in 1920 that the Foot Guards should only comprise three Regiments, pressed in 1919 and in 1921 for the formation of a Dominions Guards Regiment, to be stationed in London. Both these proposals, if accepted, would certainly have had a marked effect on the Sovereign's Birthday Parade.[31]

The central themes, however, have remained unchanged: the Troop performed by the Massed Bands, the Trooping of the Colour along the ranks of Foot Guards, and the March Past. There have, as we have seen, been alterations in detail, particularly in the part played by the Household Cavalry and in the composition of the Royal Procession, in respect of which two points are of interest: Firstly, as a result of the decision of King George V to place himself at the head of the Guards on the march to Buckingham Palace, the Birthday Parade no longer became a prelude to Guard Mounting from the

---

[31] There would also have been a marked effect on *this* and indeed on all military parades if the Holder of the Chair of Medicine at St Thomas's Hospital from 1948–63 had had his way. Writing to *The Times* on 4 July, 1951, he said: 'The erect posture in man is maintained only precariously. Standing quite still for long periods causes blood to accumulate in the lower part of the body and is equivalent to a large haemorrhage . . . "Standing to attention" introduces an additional factor since it causes obstruction to the great vein below the heart and further accumulation of blood in the lower half of the body . . . It is all the more remarkable that it should have been chosen for military ceremonial. It is, perhaps, too much to hope that we are sufficiently civilised to abandon an established tradition.'

The position of 'Stand Easy', which for many years had been accepted by the Queen's Body Guard for Scotland (The Royal Company of Archers), was altered on the advice of their Surgeon for the very reasons given above.

117

Horse Guards. And secondly, while not in any way disputing or diminishing the position and status of the Household Cavalry, the Sovereign is accompanied at the end of the Parade, with the exception of her Equerries, only by members of the Royal Family who hold appointments in the Foot Guards, Colonels of Regiments of Foot Guards and the Major General.

The Queen's 60th birthday was in 1986, which, as we have seen, was the last Parade which she attended mounted, and in uniform. In 1987, when the Colour of the 2nd Battalion Scots Guards, bearing the battle honour 'Falkland Islands', was trooped, the Commanding Officer of that Battalion was the Field Officer in Brigade Waiting, four of the eight Guards were furnished by the Regiment, and the pipes and drums of both battalions were present. The Colonel-in-Chief drove alone in an ivory mounted phaeton which had been built for Queen Victoria in 1842[32] and on this occasion it was driven by Arthur Showell, late King's Troop Royal Horse Artillery and head coachman. The horses wore Scots Guards saddle cloths and Regimental stars on their blinkers. Like her royal Father, the Queen inspected the troops in the phaeton which was driven into the courtyard of the Old Admiralty building while Her Majesty took the Salutes from a dais, with a dismounted Equerry[33] in attendance. On her return to the Palace, the Salute was again taken from a dais, and the Queen then drove into the Quadrangle escorted by the Colonels, the Major General and his ADC, the Field Officer, Master of the Horse, two Equerries and Brigade Major, all mounted.

On 24 May 1988, in the garden of Buckingham Palace, the Queen presented new Colours to the 1st Battalion Irish Guards, and it was this Queen's Colour which was trooped on 11 June. The Salute at the 2nd Rehearsal was taken by the Colonel of the Regiment, HRH The Grand Duke of Luxembourg, and, as previously, the Queen, Colonel-in-Chief, drove in her phaeton. The Colonel Scots Guards was not present as he was in Australia.

The ceremony was distinguished in many ways: It was watched from the Major General's room by the Royal Party which included King Hussein and Queen Noor of Jordan (who were also on the balcony at the Palace later), and for the first time since 1973, and probably for the last this century, all Regiments of the Foot Guards were represented on parade by at least one Guard. For the first time the Major General wore on his right shoulder the gold aiguilette with the Queen's cypher on the points—a privilege extended by Her Majesty's command 'in order to emphasise the Major General's particular responsibilities in command of the Sovereign's personal Guards'.[34]

The Lieutenant Colonels commanding Regiments of Foot Guards were on

---

[32] During World War II, it was housed in the Orangery at Windsor and subsequently restored and used twice by Her Majesty at the Windsor Horse Show, with a Royal Canadian Mounted Police Escort.

[33] Lieutenant Colonel Blair Stewart Wilson, Scots Guards, who was also in attendance at the Palace.

[34] Letter from the Comptroller, Lord Chamberlain's Office, 30 March 1988.

After the 1986 Birthday Parade the Queen's charger Burmese was retired from ceremonial duties. Leaving the Palace for the first time in a phaeton, for the 1987 Parade, Her Majesty looks across at Burmese in her more usual role of police horse. *Express Newspapers*

parade, mounted for the last time. They had, with one exception (the Senior Lieutenant Colonel, now called 'the Colonel Foot Guards') been reduced from the rank of Colonel in 1988 and as part of the economies required by the Ministry of Defence were abolished in 1989.[35]

The Queen's Colour was handed to the Ensign by Regimental Sergeant Major McEllin who, the following day, was commissioned as a Quartermaster in his Regiment. And the Brigade Major was Lieutenant Colonel Douglas Erskine Crum, the first Scots Guardsman to fill that appointment since his father 31 years previously.

But the most significant aspect was the introduction of the new rifle—SA (or Small Arms) 80—which had been carried for the first time at guard mounting at Buckingham Palace by the Irish Guards on 28 February. Because of its weight (9½ lbs) and its short length, which prevented its butt

[35] In 1869, also as an economy measure, the Lieutenant Colonels were ordered to command a battalion in addition to commanding their Regiments, but this was changed in 1875 when they relinquished their battalion responsibilities and assumed additional command of units of the Metropolitan Volunteer Corps.

being placed on the ground, arms had to be changed frequently both in the position of the 'shoulder' and the 'slope'.[36]

The Ceremony has always marked the official birthday of the Sovereign (and at one time of the Queen Consort as well), but with the disappearance of the Military Members of the Army Board and the Foreign Attachés, it has become now a more intimate occasion when the Household Troops pay a personal tribute to their Sovereign and Colonel-in-Chief. 'Your Majesty's Guards are ready to march off, Madam', are the words addressed to the Queen by the Field Officer in Brigade Waiting, followed by the moment when Her Majesty moves out on to the Parade Ground and takes position at the head of the Queen's Guard: this climax symbolises what we have stood for over the centuries and our especial position in peace and war. This Ceremony has become for all who have ever served or are serving in the Division not only the focal point of what we mean when we talk of ourselves, uniquely, as Guardsmen, but also the outward sign of the Queen's Majesty.

[36] The procedure for the Birthday Parade is laid down in detail in 'Standing Orders for the Household Division'. In a previous edition of 1899 it was ordered that arms were carried in both these positions. For example, the Escort advanced to receive the Colour at the 'Slope', but after they had halted came the order to 'Shoulder' as they trooped along the ranks. Moreover, when the Guards executed the March Past in Slow Time, they set off at the 'Slope' until the final 'Form' before the Saluting base when the order was given: 'Forward, by the Right, Shoulder Arms, Open Order.' After 'Eyes Front' came the command, 'Left Form. Forward. Slope Arms.' By 1905 the 'Shoulder' had disappeared until its reintroduction in place of the 'Slope' as we have seen, in 1960.

Appendix 1

THE ORDER OF CEREMONY
FOR TROOPING THE COLOUR
ON HORSE GUARDS·PARADE
IN CELEBRATION OF THE BIRTHDAY OF
HER MAJESTY THE QUEEN

Up to eight Guards of the Foot Guards, each comprising three officers and seventy non-commissioned officers and guardsmen, are formed up across the parade ground: Numbers 1 to 5 Guards on the West side facing the Horse Guards Building, and the remainder on the North side with their backs to the Old Admiralty Building. The Massed Bands of the Guards Division, together with the Corps of Drums and Pipes and Drums of the Battalions on parade, are formed up in front of the garden wall of 10 Downing Street. The Queen's Colour to be trooped is posted in front and to the left of Number 6 Guard, and when the line has formed the officers fall in.

Number 3 Guard opens its ranks through which Queen Elizabeth The Queen Mother drives on to Horse Guards Parade and Her Majesty is received with a Royal Salute. Number 3 Guard is reformed, and at 11 a.m. the Queen's procession arrives. This is led by the Brigade Major, Household Division, four Troopers of The Life Guards, the Massed Mounted Bands of the Household Cavalry, and the First and Second Divisions of the Sovereign's Escort.

Her Majesty is accompanied by Colonels of Foot Guards of the Blood Royal, the Field Officer and Second in Command of the Escort, the Standard Coverer, Standard Bearer and Trumpeter, Master of the Horse and the Gold Stick in Waiting. The Crown Equerry and Equerries in Waiting to the Queen are followed by other Colonels of the Household Cavalry and Foot Guards, the Major General Commanding the Household Division, Silver Stick in Waiting and members of the Major General's staff. Other officers of the Household Cavalry and Foot Guards, two Grooms of the Royal Household, four Troopers of The Blues and Royals and the Third and Fourth Divisions of the Escort complete the Procession.

Overleaf: The 1987 Birthday Parade. (*Above*) The Queen is received with a Royal Salute. On the right, mounted, are Major General Lord Michael Fitzalan Howard, Gold Stick in Waiting, and the Earl of Westmoreland, Master of the Horse. (*Below*) The Sovereign's Escort of the Household Cavalry walks past the Queen. *PRO HQ London District*

The Household Cavalry form up behind Numbers 2, 3 and 4 Guards in front of the Guards Memorial, and Her Majesty is received with a Royal Salute. The Queen, accompanied by HRH The Duke of Edinburgh and certain senior officers, then inspects the Guards and the Sovereign's Escort, and when Her Majesty has returned to the front of the Horse Guards Building, the Field Officer in Brigade Waiting, who commands the Parade, gives the command 'Troop'. The Massed Bands and Drums slow march and quick march across the ground, and during the Quick Troop one side drummer leaves the Massed Bands and marches to the right of the Line. As soon as the music stops he beats the 'Drummer's Call', upon which the command of Number 1 Guard, referred to as the 'Escort for the Colour', is taken over from the Captain by the Lieutenant.

The Escort then marches to the centre of the parade ground and halts, facing the Colour. They march to the traditional tune 'The British Grenadiers', used by all Regiments at this point of the Parade because the right flank company of every Battalion used to be a Grenadier Company. The Regimental Sergeant Major, who never draws his sword except on this one occasion, hands over the Colour to the Ensign. When the Escort presents arms to receive the Colour, the four Non-Commissioned officers at the flanks turn outwards and port arms, symbolising their protection. The Colour is then Trooped down the line of Guards and the Escort returns to its original position, the Captain resuming command.

The Guards now form up and march past in slow and quick time, and the Massed Bands play the appropriate Regimental Tunes as they pass Her Majesty. When the Guards have reformed in their original positions, the Massed Bands of the Household Cavalry move forward to the centre of the Ground, and the Sovereign's Escort walks and trots past, returning to its position when the final Royal Salute is given. The Household Cavalry then leaves Horse Guards Parade and each Guard forms into two divisions in preparation for the march to Buckingham Palace. The leading division consists of the men who will form the Queen's Guard for the day.

Queen Elizabeth The Queen Mother and other members of the Royal Family who have been watching from the windows over the Horse Guards Arch depart, and Her Majesty places herself at the head of her Guards.

At Buckingham Palace, the two detachments of the New Queen's Guard enter the Forecourt and form up opposite the Old Guard. The remaining Guards march past the Queen who takes the salute in the Centre Gateway. The King's Troop, Royal Horse Artillery, who has earlier fired a Royal Salute in Green Park, and the Sovereign's Escort, then rank past Her Majesty, after which the Queen drives into the Palace between her Old and New Guards.

Appendix 2

Of all the Guards, or Public Duties, furnished by the Foot Guards in London, the Queen's Guard is the most important and prestigious. As we have seen, the Parade marking the official birthday of the Sovereign was 'Guard Mounting and Trooping the Colour', attended in London in the reign of Queen Victoria by Her Representative and, until 1914, ended on Horse Guards when the Duties were formed up and marched off. The ceremony of mounting the Queen's (or King's) Guard then followed, and this has generally been associated with the Forecourt of Buckingham Palace. This, however, has not always been so.

Queen Victoria was the first reigning Sovereign to live there, as the building alterations which were to transform Buckingham (or King's) House into a Palace were not completed until a month before the death of William IV so that he never had an opportunity to take up residence as he had intended. Queen Victoria used it extensively up to 1861 when Prince Albert died, and while, as is explained in Appendix 3, the 'official' place of the Court was St James's Palace,[1] it is assumed that a Guard was mounted with ceremony at Buckingham Palace, though the procedure is not known.

After 1861, however, the Queen seldom went there, although members of the Royal Family kept apartments for their visits to London and the Shah of Persia stayed in 1873. The ceremony of Mounting the Queen's Guard, therefore, took place in St James's Palace.

With the accession of King Edward VII, Buckingham Palace became the Sovereign's London home and standing orders for the Brigade of Guards stated, 'Consequently the King's Guard will in future include what has hitherto been the Buckingham Palace Guard but for purposes of accommodation will be divided into the St James's Palace and Buckingham Palace Detachments.'

When neither the King nor Queen was in residence at Buckingham Palace, the King's Guard mounted with the St James's Palace detachment at St James's, and the Buckingham Palace detachment separately. When either was in residence, the ceremony took place in the Forecourt of Buckingham Palace where both detachments formed up together as the 'Old Guard'.

In the reigns of Kings George V and VI the place of Guardmounting, the procedures, the strength of detachments, the number of sentries posted, and

---

[1] The present officers' Guardroom was erected at St James's in 1793.

(*Above*) Guard Mounting, Buckingham Palace, in early 1902. This photograph, taken by HRH Princess Victoria, sister of King George V, shows that the New Guard faced the Old Guard, who were formed up in front of the Palace. *Copyright reserved. Reproduced by gracious permission of Her Majesty The Queen. (Below)* The same scene taken in 1988 from the same window of the Palace. The Band is about to form up at the end of Guard Mounting. *PRO HQ London District*

(*Above*) HRH The Prince of Wales (later Edward VIII) served in the Grenadier Guards in World War I. This picture shows him as the Ensign of the Old Guard entering Wellington Barracks after Guard Mounting. (*Below*) The Old Guard under Major Joe Vandeleur furnished by 2nd Battalion Irish Guards, 30 October 1939. *Imperial War Museum*

the Colour to be carried depended upon whether the Court was or was not deemed to be 'In Residence', and the subsequent detail outlined in Standing Orders was unbelievably complicated. It must have been a great relief to all concerned when an amendment was published in 1964 (in block letters) saying, 'the Queen's Guard will mount at Buckingham Palace throughout the year with the exception of wet weather when detachments will mount separately.'

The procedure is in fact very simple. The Old Guard is formed up in the Forecourt facing North, the St James's Palace detachment having marched down from St James's Palace with the Drums. The New Guard marches from Wellington Barracks behind their Regimental Military Band into the Forecourt, forms into line, advances towards the Old Guard, and halts. Both Guards present arms, the Captain hands over a symbolic key and the reliefs (or new sentries) are posted at both Palaces. When this has been completed, the Old Guard marches out of the Forecourt in Slow Time behind the Band, returning to Barracks, and the St James's Palace Detachment of the (new) Queen's Guard proceeds up the Mall. The Buckingham Palace Detachment marches to their Guardroom at the Palace.

During both World Wars this ceremony continued, in 1939–45 the Troops wearing battledress and steel helmets and the officers armed with revolvers. Steel plated sentry boxes were introduced and with the formation of a Westminster Garrison Battalion which also guarded Government 'key points' in Whitehall, no colour was carried.

The Queen's Guard comprises three officers, the senior of whom, regardless of rank, is 'the Captain of the Queen's Guard'. He is presented to the Queen at Investitures, before State Banquets and during Evening Diplomatic Receptions.

The whole Guard turns out and presents arms only to the Queen, the Duke of Edinburgh, Queen Elizabeth the Queen Mother and the Prince of Wales if accompanied by an Escort.

The Buckingham Palace Detachment acts similarly to the same members of the Royal Family and Heads of Commonwealth and Foreign States on official occasions; when the Queen departs for, and returns from, overseas journeys when Ministers are present; on the occasion of a private visit to Buckingham Palace of a Commonwealth or Foreign Head of State; and to the St James's Palace Detachment with uncased Colours.

Sentries of the Queen's Guard who, at Buckingham Palace, used to be posted outside the railings until the crowds made it impossible for them to patrol their beats, resulting in them being moved into the Forecourt, are instructed to recognise the members of the Royal Family and their cars in order to pay the correct compliment.[2]

[2] Paragraph 24 of Standing Orders for the Brigade of Guards, 1899, reads: 'Sentries will present arms to Royal carriages with two footmen whether in red or drab coats, without endeavouring to ascertain who is inside, as none but the Royal Family have two footmen. The Royal Servants, when not in full dress liveries or greatcoats, wear a red cord over the shoulder.'

127

Appendix 3

THE HORSE GUARDS BUILDING AND PARADE
A SHORT HISTORY

The present Horse Guards building dates from the mid-eighteenth century, but it stands on a site where, since 1245, the Archbishops of York had their official residence until 1529 when Henry VIII usurped Cardinal Wolsey and appropriated his palace. The King extended it so that it stretched almost from Charing Cross to Westminster, and he acquired as a private hunting ground the parkland of St James's, encircling it with a high brick wall and building a hunting lodge which is now St James's Palace. Occupying the present site of Horse Guards was a Tiltyard for jousting which was completed by 1533.

The first military building associated with the King's Palace was built in the reign of Charles I to house the Royal Guards and to provide a security force. In December 1641 the Surveyor of Works was ordered to 'build a Court of Guards in the Tiltyard before Whitehall', and it was immediately to the south that Cromwell established the main administrative centre for his military regime. From this beginning the Tiltyard, and later Horse Guards on the same site, was to remain the sole focus of military authority for the next 250 years.

After the restoration of the monarchy the old Cromwellian guardhouse and offices were demolished, but the original Tiltyard walls were repaired, and between them in 1663–4 was built the 'Old Horse Guards' building, taking its name from the continual presence there of the officers and men of the Troops of Horse Guards. The layout was similar to that of the present building—an enclosed courtyard on the Whitehall side and a central clocktower block through which a large gateway gave access to St James's Park.

Another building was added to the southern end to house the detachments of Foot Guards and, to differentiate in written orders between the two Guards, that of the Foot Guards was called 'The Tiltyard Guard'[1] while that of the Household Cavalry was termed 'The Horse Guards Guard'.

Old Horse Guards was the only purpose-built Military Headquarters in London, housing not only the Regimental Headquarters of the Household Cavalry and Foot Guards but also military departments which eventually formed the War Office.

On the morning of 5 January, 1698, as the diarist John Evelyn records,

---

[1] The Tiltyard Guard continued until its last mounting in November 1898.

128

'Whitehall burnt, nothing but walls and ruins left'. Apart from the Banqueting Hall and Old Horse Guards, the entire Palace was destroyed, and the King decided that St James's would be the official residence of the Court, with Old Horse Guards Arch as the only official entrance.[2] Various plans were made to rebuild Whitehall Palace but none was executed.

Old Horse Guards gradually deteriorated to such an extent that Gold Stick, Lord de la Warre, Lord Cardigan and the Judge Advocate General wrote to the Secretary-at-War on 3 May, 1745: 'The whole building belonging to the Horse Guards being in a very rotten and decayed condition ... it is now become so dangerous that it is not safe for the coaches of His Majesty and the Royal Family to pass under the gateway.'[3] As a result the decision to rebuild was made and William Kent's design accepted. On 5 September, 1749, the Board of Works submitted Kent's drawings to the Treasury for approval, accompanied by a description which included the following extracts: 'In the Principal or Middle Building there may be a room for the holding of Courts Martial, a Chapel and an office for the Secretary-at-War ... with two rooms for the officers of the Horse Guards ... On the South side of the Middle Building and Court is proposed a Guardroom and rooms for the officers of the Foot Guards, larger and better than they are now ...'[4] The estimate of total cost was £31,748.

On 24 April 1750 the Chancellor of the Exchequer directed the Board to proceed 'taking care to use as little of the Park as possible', and the work was completed by 1760.[5] Contemporary criticism was mainly directed at the lack of grandeur of the building and in particular that the archway was not befitting the principal Palace entrance. Before the State Opening of Parliament in 1762 the *London Chronicle* reported that 'the ground is going to be lowered under the arch ... to make room for His Majesty's new state coach to pass through.'[6]

By 1803 the building was packed with the offices of Secretaries of State, the

[2] Ambassadors are today accredited to 'the Court of St James' and passage except on foot through Horse Guards Arch is restricted to holders of a Special Ivory Pass.

[3] PRO WO 4/40.

[4] PRO Works 6/17.

[5] PRO T29/31. Although accounts for the period June 1753 to March 1754 are missing, the recorded expenditure totalled about £45,000.

[6] The 6th Duke of Portland recalled the following: 'Before the coronation (of Edward VII) I had a remarkable dream. A State Coach had to pass through the Arch at the Horse Guards on the way to Westminster Abbey. I dreamed that it stuck in the Arch and that some of the Life Guards on duty were compelled to hew off the crown upon the coach before it could be freed. When I told the Crown Equerry, Colonel Evans, he laughed and said, "What do dreams matter?" "At all events," I replied, "let us have the coach and arch measured." So this was done and to my astonishment we found the arch was nearly two feet too low to allow the coach to pass through.'

Commander-in-Chief and many other officers and officials, and extra accommodation was created by adding two more storeys to the blocks connecting the wings to the centre, as a result of which it acquired the curved appearance that is has today.

Before the advent in 1859 of Big Ben, the Horse Guards clock was accepted as London's most famous and reliable timepiece. The present clock was made in 1768, and the hour bell and its two quarterly chimes were cast and hung in 1789. The Sovereign's arrival at the Saluting base for the Birthday Parade is precisely timed as this clock strikes eleven.

Public Buildings of London by Brittan and Pugin included in 1825 an interior plan of Horse Guards which showed some interesting changes, the most notable of which were that the room over the archway facing Whitehall, originally the Chapel,[7] had become the office of the Commander-in-Chief; the room opposite, overlooking the Parade Ground, previously the Court Martial

---

[7] The place of worship for the Household Troops became the gallery pews in the Banqueting Hall until 1839 when the Guards Chapel, Wellington Barracks, was first built.

The Duke of Wellington, Commander-in-Chief, interviewing a mother about her son, in what is now the Major General's office. The desk is that still in use, and this picture is in the office. *PRO HQ London District*

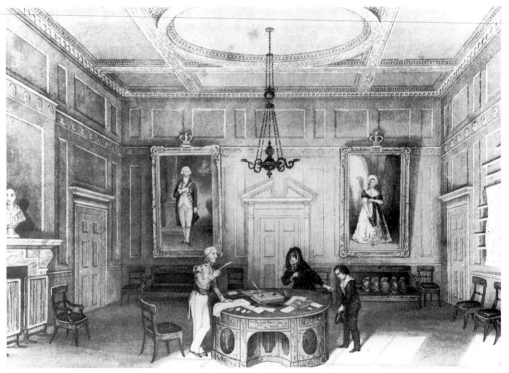

Room, was now the Audience Room (sometimes later called the Levee Room, and presently the office of the Major General from which members of the Royal Family watch the ceremony). The accommodation for the Foot Guards Headquarters is shown on the ground floor.

In 1855 the Secretary of State and his civil staff left for 81–91 Pall Mall, known as Buckingham House, outside which sentries from the Queen's Guard were posted. The Commander-in-Chief, HRH the Duke of Cambridge, reluctantly followed in 1870 but in a gesture of defiance he continued to head his letters 'Horse Guards, Pall Mall'. A purpose-built War Office was built in Whitehall between 1899 and 1906 to accommodate the entire centralised control of the Army, thus leaving the Horse Guards building as a Headquarters for the Troops in London, the Household Cavalry and Foot Guards.

With the exception of the periods of the two World Wars,[8] the Major General and his staff have been located there, but at a date still to be determined extensive work to the fabric and interior will force a move of all the offices to Chelsea Barracks until completed.

Horse Guards Parade
The Parade once had many trees surrounding it but these were gradually removed to allow more space for military ceremonial. On 18 January, 1816, two standards with eagles, captured from the French at Waterloo, were lodged in the Banqueting Hall.[9] They were carried across the Ground and through the Arch in a procession headed by the band of the Grenadier Guards and followed by a detachment of Life Guards, two Sergeants of the Grenadier and Coldstream Guards carrying the trophies, and detachments of the three regiments of Foot Guards bringing up the rear.

Following the Napoleonic Wars, thought was given to constructing a National Shrine in honour of fallen servicemen, and in three of the most imaginative schemes Horse Guards was to be the focal point of the proposed Place d'Armées. No illustration survives of the earliest—'A Triumphal Entrance to the Horse Guards designed to commemorate the Services of the Deceased', exhibited by W. Wilkins at the Royal Academy in 1837, but plans by Sir Charles Barry (1845) and Alfred Beaumont (1850) exist.

The Duke of Wellington's funeral procession in 1852 started from there, and in 1853 Queen Victoria presented Crimean medals.

Sited about where the Guards Memorial now stands[10] was the 'St James

[8] In 1864 the Guards Division office was at Wellington Barracks. The 1899 and 1905 editions of Standing Orders for the Brigade of Guards were issued from 'The Brigade Office, 23 Carlton House Terrace', while the 1911 and subsequent editions showed that Headquarters had moved to Horse Guards.
[9] Converted at this time into a chapel.
[10] Unveiled by HRH the Duke of Connaught at a large Parade, 16 October, 1926.

Alfred Beaumont's design for a new Triumphal Entrance to Horse Guards Parade. 1850.
Copyright reserved. Reproduced by gracious permission of Her Majesty The Queen.

Milk Fair' which had dispensed milk from cows which grazed nearby since the days of Charles II. In the 1880s there were over a dozen tethered cows, but they were steadily reduced to two when, in February 1905, the milkmaids, Miss Kitchen and Miss Burns, departed 'towards Leicester Square'.

W. Speaight exhibited a scheme in 1909 but it does not seem to have been seriously considered. Nonetheless, some individual memorials are on the Ground: Viscount Wellesley (1917) Earl Roberts (1923) and Earl Kitchener (1926).

Horse Guards Parade has since 1945 been the site for Presentations of Colours, Royal Reviews, the 150th anniversary of the Battle of Waterloo, *Son et Lumière*, and a Review of the Household Troops, under the command of the Major General for President de Gaulle. Its fame, however, remains in its magnificent setting for the Soveriegn's Birthday Parade which will not be disturbed by the impending work on Horse Guards Building.

132

Appendix 4

The Brigade of Guards

Until 1856 all orders for the Foot Guards were issued by the Field Officer in Brigade Waiting, an appointment in the Royal Household filled by a senior officer of one of the Regiments in rotation. On 14 July 1856 the following Brigade order was published:

> Her Majesty has been pleased to appoint Major General Lord Rokeby, KCB, to serve on the staff of the Army, with a view to his exercising a general supervision over Battalions in England, including Aldershot; all communications having reference to the Brigade of Guards will be addressed to him in future, instead of the Field Officer in Brigade Waiting as before.

Lord Rokeby, who had fought at Waterloo aged 17 and who, when he died in 1883 as 20th Colonel of the Scots Guards and the last of those before whose names the Waterloo 'W' was affixed in the Army List, was thus the first Major General.

However, for some years afterwards the Field Officer continued to exercise considerable control over the military affairs of what was then known as 'The Brigade of Guards', the Major General issuing General Orders, the details of which the Field Officer carried out.

Between 1856 and 1868 the Foot Guards were called a 'Division', but on 27 April 1868 the old term 'Brigade' was restored, and it was then laid down that the Major General's orders should be called 'Brigade Orders' and those of the Field Officer 'Sub Brigade Orders'. The Home District (now London District) was created in 1870 and placed under the command of the Major General Commanding the Brigade of Guards, and on 28 February 1873 the Sub Brigade Office was abolished.

The Household Brigade

By 1950 London District had ceased to be an independent District and had come under the command of Headquarters Eastern Command. However, in his capacity as Major General Commanding the Brigade of Guards, the Major General remained an Independent Commander under the War Office, to which he had direct access on all subjects peculiar to the Brigade. This is still the case and today the Major General continues to have direct access to the Ministry of Defence on subjects peculiar to the Household Division.

In December 1950 King George VI directed that the Household Cavalry should come under the Major General's Command and that the latter should be known in future as the Major General Commanding the Household Brigade. It was not, however, until 12 June 1952 that the title of Brigade Major, Brigade of Guards, which had come into being on 27 June 1861, was changed to Brigade Major, Household Brigade.

The Household Division

Early in 1967 the Ministry of Defence decided to form the Infantry of the Line into larger groupings to be known as Divisions, in preparation for the cuts in the Defence Services then being planned by the Government. As a result, on 1 July 1968 the Household Brigade became the Household Division and the Brigade of Guards the Guards Division, and the Major General's title was changed to Major General Commanding the Household Division.

The Senior Colonel, Household Division

The appointment of Senior Colonel is held by the Colonel who has been in office for the longest time in the Household Division. HRH the Duke of Edinburgh is the Senior Colonel, and in 1971, when he was acting in the place of HRH the late Duke of Gloucester, who was ill, he established the custom of holding a conference at Buckingham Palace, followed by dinner the evening before the Birthday Parade. All the Colonels attend, as does the Major General.

The Senior Colonel advises the Sovereign on matters of policy concerning the Division, taking into account the advice of the Colonels and the Major General. Her Majesty's Regulations for the Household Division, first published for the Brigade of Guards in 1853, are issued over his signature.

Photos opposite: *PRO HQ London District*

Appendix 5

The Regimental Bands

The Military (or Regimental) Bands of the Foot Guards trace their origins to Charles II who, during his exile in France, admired the sound of the 'hautboy', a type of oboe. On the restoration of the Monarchy and shortly before he died, the King issued a warrant in 1685 authorising twelve hautboys in the King's Regiment of Foot Guards.[1]

During the first half of the eighteenth century a wider range of instruments was introduced replacing the hautboys, as described by Parke:[2]

> The bands of the three regiments of Guards about the year 1785 consisted of only eight performers, viz: two oboes, two clarinets, two French horns, and two bassoons, selected from the King's and patent theatres. They were excellent performers on their several instruments, were hired by the month, and were well paid. They were not attested, and were exempt from all Military duties except that of King's Guard which they played from the parade at Horse Guards in St James's Park to the courtyard of the (St James's) Palace one morning, and back again from the Palace to the Horse Guards on the following day.

Of these musicians Burney wrote,[3] 'If I had the inclination to describe in a pompous manner merely the effects of wind instruments in martial music, there had been no occasion to quit London: for at St James's and in the Park, every morning we have now an excellent band; and hitherto, as I have not seen more soldier-like men in any service than our own, so the music and musicians of other places, exceeding ours in nothing but the number and variety of the instruments.'

When in 1789 Lord William Cathcart transfered from a Regiment of the Line into the Coldstream Guards as a Lieutenant Colonel, he was unaware that the engagement of the Band was very different from that of the Regiment which he had left. On one occasion he required them to play for him and a party of his friends during an excursion down the river to Greenwich. As this

---

[1] See also Footnote 5.

[2] William Thomas Parke, *Musical memories 1784–1830*. London, 1830 (BL Shelfmark 1042. H. 26).

[3] Charles Burney, *The Present State of Music in Germany, etc*. London, T. Becker & Co., 1773 (BL Shelfmark 129 A 26,27).

A re-enactment of Guard Mounting in the 1790s, by the 1st Battalion Coldstream Guards in 1932. The Old and New Guards face each other in St James's Palace with the Band on the left. The Time Beaters and Drummer Boys are clearly visible. *RHQ Coldstream Guards*

A member of the Band of the 3rd Guards (now Scots Guards) by E. Hull. This picture was annotated by General Sir J. Aitchison when the Lieutenant Colonel Commanding the Regiment, 'I believe this correct. At this date there is no tambourine in the Band, only one Black whose dress is the same as this only he had a red waistcoat. 1839.' *RHQ Scots Guards*

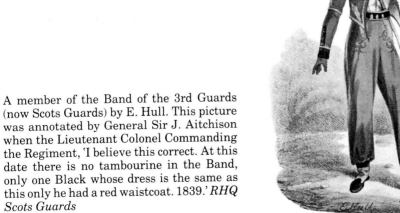

137

request clashed with the private engagements of the musicians, they declined. The officers, who subscribed to pay the Band, were upset and wrote to HRH The Duke of York, Colonel of the Regiment, who at the time was in Germany, saying that they wanted a band which they could command on all occasions. The Duke agreed and a German band was formed and sent to England to supersede the British musicians. It consisted of twenty-four instrumentalists—clarinets, oboes, french horns, flutes, bassoons, trumpets, trombones and serpents.[4] The band included three coloured men called 'Time Beaters'[5] who played drums, tambourines and turkish bells, sometimes called 'Jingling Johnny'. They were dressed in Eastern clothes and plumed turbans, and were retained until nearly the middle of the nineteenth century.[6]

Shortly before the three Regimental Bands visited Paris after the Battle of Waterloo, the 'Kent' key bugle was introduced, which caused a sensation in the French capital. On return to London a reorganisation took place: the hired professional musicians were replaced by men who enlisted into their respective Regiments. Each band now consisted of twenty-two performers who, like the 'Hautboys' of old, wore state uniforms similar to those worn today by the Drum Majors of the Foot Guards and the bands of the Household Cavalry.[7] Carl Boose became Bandmaster[8] of the Scots Guards in 1842 and introduced new instruments. There was then a period of little change from about 1845 until the end of the century when the saxophone, which had been invented in 1840, began to be recognised in England and gradually replaced the alto and bass clarinets.

The Band of the Irish Guards was formed at the same time as the Regiment was raised in 1900, consisting of 35 musicians under a Warrant officer Bandmaster, and five years later made the first of many tours of Canada which included performing at the Canadian National Exhibition in 1911.

[4] The bass member of the zinke family. It had been used for many years in Germany for giving alarm in case of fire and, in war, the approach of the enemy.

[5] To this day, as a result, the Bass Drummer in the Regimental Band of the Grenadier Guards is called, uniquely, 'Time Beater'. After the death of Charles II he wore a black armband in permanent mourning for the King. This ceased when the ornate musician's tunic was not reintroduced after the Second World War. In Mrs. Pappendick's book, *Court and Private Life in the Time of Queen Charlotte*, referred to by Captain F. W. Wood, Director of Music Scots Guards, 1909–1929 in an article in the *Household Brigade Magazine*, Spring 1929, it is recorded that in 1788: 'One circumstance greatly disturbed and vexed the king, and it is feared brought forward his direful malady to a more violent crisis, was the return of the Duke of York from Hanover, without permission, and the unceasing endeavours of HRH to persuade The King to allow him to introduce into the Guards' bands the Turkish musical instruments ...'

[6] John Baptist was the last Time Beater to serve in the Scots Guards and was discharged on 22nd December, 1841.

[7] Except for the Drum Majors, this uniform was discontinued in 1832 in the Foot Guards.

[8] Until 1825 the conductors of the Coldstream Band had been German. In that year Charles Godfrey, who had joined as a musician in 1813, was appointed and served till he died in 1863 when he was succeeded by his son who retired in 1880.

A Foot Guards Band at St James's Palace circa 1796, by Thomas Stothard. *Reproduced by Courtesy of the Trustees of the British Museum*

The Welsh Guards Band was formed in October, 1915, and performed their first duty on St David's Day, 1916, at Guard Mounting, followed the same day by a Welsh Patriotic Meeting at the London Opera House. At the Great Victory Parade in Paris at the end of World War I they led the Colour Parties of the British Army through the Arc de Triomphe.

During the Second World War, on 18th June 1944, the Band of the Coldstream Guards was playing at Divine Service in the Guards' Chapel, Wellington Barracks, when the Chapel was struck by a German V1 flying bomb, killing more than 120 people including Major Windram, Senior Director of Music, and five musicians.

The establishment of a Foot Guards Band up to April 1985 was one Director of Music and 59 Musicians. As a manpower economy measure the Ministry of Defence ordered a reduction to one and 50, and for the Birthday Parade each furnishes a Director and 47.[9]

---

[9] Each Household Cavalry Band was established at one and 39. This was similarly reduced to one and 35 and they parade massed at a strength of one Director, two Drum Horses and 56 Musicians.

The precise split in instrumentation is decided by individual Directors, but the following is a guide:

Flute/Piccolo	2	Horn	4
Eb Clarinet	1	Bb Cornet	8
Oboe	2	Tenor Trombone	5
Bb Clarinet	11	Bass Trombone	2
Eb Alto Saxophone	2	Euphonium	2
Bb Tenor Saxophone	2	Tuba	4
Bassoon	2	Percussion	3

When massed, as for The Queen's Birthday Parade in 1988, the major instruments numerically are: 49 cornets; 45 clarinets; 20 Trombones and 20 Horns, forming the front and seventh ranks respectively on a frontage of twenty musicians.

The Programme of Music is submitted by the Major General to the Queen's Private Secretary for Her Majesty's approval or comments. Many of the tunes are established and regularly played: 'Les Huguenots' (the Slow Troop by the Massed Bands), 'The British Grenadiers' (as the Escort for the Colour advances), the 'Grenadiers' Slow March' (as the Colour is Trooped), the Slow and Quick Marches of the Regiments of Foot Guards and the Slow March and Regiment's Trot of the Regiments of Household Cavalry. There are, however, two marches which are played by the Massed Bands during the Inspection of the Line by the Queen,[10] the Quick Troop, 'Neutral' Slow and Quick Marches before and after the Guards pass Her Majesty on the Saluting dais, as there is 'Neutral' Walk Past and Trot for the Household Cavalry. The Pipes and Drums play the Massed Bands as they move back to the South of the Ground after the March Past, and during the return down the Mall to the Palace there are three tunes played by the Pipes and Drums, a march by the Corps of Drums, and two by the Bands. Finally the Massed Bands perform a selection of about six tunes in the Forecourt of the Palace at the end of the Ceremony.

The Corps of Drums and Pipes and Drums
Unlike the Infantry of the Line which has military *battalion* bands, the Foot Guards, as we have seen, have military *regimental* bands. On the other hand, each Guards battalion has a drum and fife band, known as the Corps of Drums, and, uniquely among the Scottish and Irish infantry, the Scots and Irish Guards battalions *also* have pipe bands—referred to as the Pipes and Drums.

On the Birthday Parade, whenever one of these regiments is represented in the Guards, the Corps of Drums or Pipes and Drums are present, massed with the Bands, and sometimes both. For instance, in 1988, when every Regiment

[10] Section V of Household Division Standing Orders contains a heading, 'Precautions', beneath which is written the following: '*Horses* (para)1005. Bands and Drums are to play pianissimo where necessary to avoid frightening horses.' Failure to comply with this order has contributed to an increase in membership of the Empty Saddle Club.

of Foot Guards was represented, the massed Corps of Drums paraded with twenty-seven side and four bass drummers, four cymbal players and forty-five flautists.[11] The Pipes and Drums of the 2nd Battalion Scots Guards and 1st Battalion Irish Guards mustered twenty-six pipers and fourteen side drummers. The total of 120 made up the six rear ranks of the Massed Bands.

In early days, in peace and war, the drums and those who beat them were extremely important: The drummer beat out the Commander's orders to the front line; kept his drum rolling to tell the troops the Colours were safe; walked fearlessly towards the enemy to seek a parley; raised morale on the march, and in garrison beat the camp calls.[12] The Fife came into service during the early sixteenth century, and although its popularity varied, the Duke of Cumberland, Commander-in-Chief of the British Army and of the allied forces in Flanders in 1747, ordered the British Foot Guards to have drumbeating accompanied by fifes when they were in camp in Maastricht. Later, however, in the Crimean War, Lord Raglan banned military music, to little avail as Russell, *The Times* correspondent at the Seat of War, related that the Drums and Fifes of the Foot Guards 'kept the whole place alive last night and cheered the drenched rifle picquets far above the bay on the misty mountain tops.'

The Drummers are trained to sound bugle calls and all carry bugles on parade. When a battalion of Foot Guards changes station and moves from its

[11] On this occasion the 2nd Battalion Scots Guards only furnished their Pipes and Drums.
[12] See *The Drum* by Hugh Barty-King, published 1988 by The Royal Tournament.

Pipers of the 1st Battalion Irish Guards, 1917. *Imperial War Museum*

barracks, instead of the Guard (or Duty) Drummer rousing the sleepers, the whole Corps of Drums marches round the Lines sounding the 'Long Reveille'.

Before 1856 there were no pipers on the regimental establishment of the Scots Guards, although some company commanders provided themselves with them unofficially and at their own expense.[13] In 1853 a pipe major was appointed, again unofficially, by the 1st Battalion during the Crimean War, but three years later a Pipe Major and five pipers were authorised for each of the two battalions. From that time to the present day the number of established pipers has increased and the high standard of performance become widely recognised.

As pipers in battle, Irish pipers have a very long history. They crossed over into Gascony in 1286 in the cause of Edward I and they were at Crécy in 1346. Like the Scots bagpipe, the Irish warpipe was considered provocative. Edward III banned it and Cromwell threatened those who played it with banishment to Barbados. The pipes and drums of the Irish Guards were formed in 1916 and carried the warpipe until 1960, when they adopted the Scots instrument with the extra drone.

On the Birthday Parade, when the Colour of either Regiment is Trooped, the pipers move forward, form a single rank in front of the Massed Bands and play the Escort past the Queen in quick time to the respective Regimental March.

[13] 'With us any Captain may keep a piper in his company and maintain him, too, for no pay is allowed him, perhaps just as much as he deserveth.' *Pallas Armata*, Sir James Turner, 1670/71.

Appendix 6

THE SOVEREIGN'S BIRTHDAY PARADE
1895 TO 1989

Year	Date	Escort	Salute taken by	Remarks
1895	Fri 24 May	1st Scots Gds	HM Queen Victoria	At Windsor Castle
1895	Sat 25 May	2nd Scots Gds	HRH The Prince of Wales	At Horse Guards Parade
1896	Wed 20 May	2nd Grenadier Gds	HRH The Prince of Wales	
1897	Mon 24 May	2nd Coldstream Gds	HRH The Prince of Wales	
1898	Sat 21 May	1st Coldstream Gds	HRH The Prince of Wales	
1899	Sat 3 June	2nd Coldstream Gds	HRH The Prince of Wales	
1900	Wed 23 May	1st Grenadier Gds	HRH The Prince of Wales	
1901	Fri 24 May	3rd Scots Gds	HM King Edward VII	} Combined with presentation
1902	Fri 30 May	1st Irish Gds	HM The King	} of the Colours
1903	Fri 26 June	2nd Coldstream Gds	HM The King	
1904	Tue 24 June	3rd Coldstream Gds	HRH The Prince of Wales	The King visiting Germany
1905	—	—	—	Parade cancelled (weather)
1906	—	—	—	Parade cancelled (weather)
1907	Fri 28 June	1st Irish Gds	HM The King	
1908	Sat 26 June	1st Coldstream Gds	HM The King	
1909	—	—	—	Parade cancelled (weather)
1910	—	—	—	No Parade (Court Mourning)
1911	—	—	—	No Parade (Coronation of George V)
1912	Fri 14 June	1st Grenadier Gds	HM King George V	
1913	Tue 3 June	2nd Scots Gds	HM The King	
1914	Fri 22 June	1st Grenadier Gds	HM The King	

THE FIRST WORLD WAR

Year	Date	Escort	Salute taken by	Remarks
1919	Tue 3 June	3rd Coldstream Gds	HM The King	In Hyde Park
1920	Sat 5 June	1st Grenadier Gds	HM The King	In Hyde Park
1921	Sat 4 June	1st Grenadier Gds	HM The King	At Horse Guards Parade
1922	Sat 3 June	1st Coldstream Gds	HM The King	
1923	Sat 2 June	2nd Scots Gds	HM The King	
1924	Tue 3 June	2nd Grenadier Gds	HM The King	
1925	Wed 3 June	1st Irish Gds	HM The King	
1926	—	—	—	No Parade (General Strike)
1927	Sat 4 June	3rd Grenadier Gds	HM The King	
1928	Mon 4 June	1st Welsh Gds	HM The King	
1929	Mon 3 June	3rd Coldstream Gds	HRH The Duke of Connaught	The King was ill
1930	Tue 3 June	2nd Scots Gds	HRH The Prince of Wales	The King was ill
1931	Sat 6 June	2nd Coldstream Gds	HM The King	
1932	Sat 4 June	2nd Grenadier Gds	HM The King	
1933	Sat 3 June	3rd Coldstream Gds	HM The King	
1934	Mon 4 June	1st Scots Gds	HM The King	
1935	Mon 3 June	1st Irish Gds	HM The King	
1936	Tue 23 June	1st Grenadier Gds	HM King Edward VIII	King Edward VIII's only Parade
1937	Wed 9 June	1st Coldstream Gds	HM King George VI	
1938	Thu 9 June	2nd Scots Gds	HM The King	
1939	Thu 8 June	2nd Grenadier Gds	HRH The Duke of Gloucester	The King was in Canada and USA

Year	Date	Escort	Salute taken by	Remarks
			THE SECOND WORLD WAR	
1947	Thu 12 June	2nd Coldstream Gds	HM The King	
1948	—	—	—	Parade cancelled (weather)
1949	Thu 9 June	1st Welsh Gds	HM The King	
1950	Thu 8 June	3rd Coldstream Gds	HM The King	
1951	Thu 7 June	3rd Grenadier Gds	HRH The Princess Elizabeth	The King was ill
1952	Thu 5 June	2nd Scots Gds	HM Queen Elizabeth II	
1953	Thu 11 June	1st Grenadier Gds	HM The Queen	
1954	Thu 10 June	1st Coldstream Gds	HM The Queen	
1955	—	—	—	Parade cancelled (National rail strike)
1956	Thu 31 May	3rd Grenadier Gds	HM The Queen	
1957	Thu 13 June	1st Irish Gds	HM The Queen	
1958	Thu 12 June	1st Scots Gds	HM The Queen	
1959	Sat 13 June	3rd Coldstream Gds	HM The Queen	Start of regular Saturday Parades
1960	Sat 11 June	3rd Grenadier Gds	HM The Queen	
1961	Sat 10 June	2nd Scots Gds	HM The Queen	
1962	Sat 2 June	2nd Coldstream Gds	HM The Queen	
1963	Sat 8 June	2nd Grenadier Gds	HM The Queen	
1964	Sat 13 June	1st Coldstream Gds	HM The Queen	
1965	Sat 12 June	1st Welsh Gds	HM The Queen	
1966	Sat 11 June	1st Irish Gds	HM The Queen	
1967	Sat 10 June	1st Grenadier Gds	HM The Queen	
1968	Sat 8 June	2nd Coldstream Gds	HM The Queen	
1969	Sat 14 June	1st Scots Gds	HM The Queen	
1970	Sat 13 June	2nd Scots Gds	HM The Queen	
1971	Sat 12 June	2nd Grenadier Gds	HM The Queen	
1972	Sat 3 June	1st Coldstream Gds	HM The Queen	'Silence' for HRH the Duke of Windsor
1973	Sat 2 June	1st Welsh Gds	HM The Queen	
1974	Sat 15 June	1st Irish Gds	HM The Queen	
1975	Sat 14 June	1st Grenadier Gds	HM The Queen	
1976	Sat 12 June	2nd Coldstream Gds	HM The Queen	
1977	Sat 11 June	1st Scots Gds	HM The Queen	
1978	Sat 3 June	2nd Grenadier Gds	HM The Queen	
1979	Sat 16 June	2nd Scots Gds	HM The Queen	
1980	Sat 14 June	1st Irish Gds	HM The Queen	
1981	Sat 13 June	1st Welsh Gds	HM The Queen	
1982	Sat 12 June	1st Coldstream Gds	HM The Queen	'Silence' for the Falklands Task Force
1983	Sat 11 June	1st Grenadier Gds	HM The Queen	
1984	Sat 16 June	2nd Grenadier Gds	HM The Queen	
1985	Sat 15 June	2nd Coldstream Gds	HM The Queen	
1986	Sat 14 June	1st Scots Gds	HM The Queen	Last Parade when the Queen was mounted
1987	Sat 13 June	2nd Scots Gds	HM The Queen	
1988	Sat 11 June	1st Irish Gds	HM The Queen	
1989	Sat 17 June	1st Coldstream Gds	HM The Queen	

144